SUPERNATURAL HORIZONS FROM GLORY TO GLORY

by Charles and Frances Hunter

Published by Hunter Books
City of Light
201 McClellan Road
Kingwood, Texas 77339, U.S.A.

BOOKS BY CHARLES FRANCES HUNTER

A CONFESSION A DAY KEEPS THE DEVIL AWAY
ANGELS ON ASSIGNMENT
BORN AGAIN! WHAT DO YOU MEAN?
COME ALIVE
DELIGHTFULLY CHARISMATIC Christian Walk Seminar
   Manual
DEVIL, YOU CAN'T STEAL WHAT'S MINE
DON'T LIMIT GOD
DON'T PANIC ... PRAY!
FOLLOW ME
GOD IS FABULOUS
GOD'S ANSWER TO FAT ... LOØSE IT!
GOD'S BIG "IF"
GOD'S CONDITIONS FOR PROSPERITY
HOT LINE TO HEAVEN
HOW TO DEVELOP YOUR FAITH
HOW TO FIND GOD'S WILL FOR YOUR LIFE
HOW TO HAVE FREEDOM FROM FEAR
HOW TO HEAL THE SICK
HOW TO MAKE YOUR MARRIAGE EXCITING
IMPOSSIBLE MIRACLES
IN JESUS' NAME!
INVEST YOUR LIFE IN GOD
IT'S SO SIMPLE (formerly HANG LOOSE WITH JESUS)
JOY, JOY, JOY!
LET'S GO WITNESSING (formerly GO, MAN! GO)
MEMORIZING MADE EASY
MY LOVE AFFAIR WITH CHARLES
NUGGETS OF TRUTH
P.T.L.A. (Praise the Lord, Anyway!)
SIMPLE AS A, B, C.
SINCE JESUS PASSED BY
SHOUT THE WORD
the fabulous SKINNIE MINNIE RECEIPE BOOK
SUPERNATURAL HORIZONS (from Glory to Glory)
THE DEVIL WANTS YOUR MIND
THE TWO SIDES OF A COIN
THIS WAY UP!
WHY SHOULD "I" SPEAK IN TONGUES???

Scripture quotations are taken from:
The Authorized King James Version (KJV)
The Living Bible, Paraphrased (TLB), © *1971 by Tyndale*
   House Publishers, Wheaton, Illinois.
The Amplified Old Testament (Amp.), © *1965 by Zondervan*
   Publishing
The Amplified New Testament (Amp.), © *The Lockman*
   Foundation 1954, 1958.
The Holy Bible, New King James Version
   Copyright © *1979, 1980, 1982 by Thomas Nelson, Inc.*
   All references are to this version unless otherwise stated.

ISBN 0-917726-52-9

TABLE OF CONTENTS

For information about the City of Light School of Ministry, Video Bible School, audio or video teaching tapes or seminar tapes, write to:

HUNTER BOOKS
City of Light
201 McClellan Road
Kingwood, Texas 77339

In the event your Christian Bookstore does not have any of the books written by Charles and Frances Hunter, please write for price list or order from Hunter Books.

CHAPTER 1

SPIRIT PERSPECTIVE
By Charles

Picture yourself high above the earth with eyes which could see vividly clear everything for millions of miles. Then picture eyes which were not limited to direction as our earthly eyes are, but which can see in all directions at the same time. Picture yourself with the ability to fly at the speed of light so you could transcend universes and cover all the earth in the twinkling of an eye.

The Spirit realm is a dimension not yet given to man, but angels view it routinely. God and Jesus made it all and they can see it all at one time. God's Spirit monitors everything on earth so He sees everything at once. There are no clouds to cover His view, nor does darkness hamper or dim His visibility.

Communication in the heavenly realm does not require sentence nor word structure, but can be transmitted with full comprehension as a flash of lightning.

God can flash a thought in a microsecond into the mind of mankind and it will take days, weeks, months, or even years to fathom its meanings in fulness, and yet it can be so simply focused into our minds that we can receive and understand lengthy messages instantly. Voices as we know them are unnecessary and even cumbersome in the divine limitlessness of communications by the Spirit of God.

God made the earth and all that is in it by speaking it into existence, so for Him to create new parts for bodies, prepare banquets for millions, extend life for eternity, burn into our minds the whole of the Bible and all its vast meanings which extend from the beginning to the end, He has but to desire to do so and it will be so.

I discovered by a dimension of the Spirit God has given to me that I could see in all directions at one time. It's not like having eyes which can see the equator around the earth, but which can see a million equator circles in all directions around the earth.

I was speaking from the lecturn on the stage of a large auditorium when I said to Frances, "I'm going to tell the people where our big angel is." Frances was sitting on the stage to my left and she thought, "Oh, God, don't let him embarrass himself. He can't see the angel from the position he is standing, because the angel's in back of him!"

I said to the audience, "The angel is standing directly in back of me, his back is about three feet from the drapes, he is about fifteen feet in back of me and he is looking directly over my head at the audience."

I physically did not see him as often angels are

seen, but in the Spirit dimension I could sense where he was. I didn't look around, I didn't move my eyes, but with those limitless spirit eyes I knew exactly where he stood.

We believe, to a great extent, that we citizens of this earth who are also citizens of the Kingdom of God will move in the limitlessness of the Spirit realm in this last generation before Jesus returns. Nothing is impossible with God, so nothing should be impossible for God to do through us.

There is only one true God and we are to worship Him only, and we give all glory to Him through Jesus whom God sent to earth as His highest glory.

"But You, O Lord, are a shield for me, My glory and the One who lifts up my head" (Psalms 3:3).

"O Lord, our Lord, How excellent is Your name in all the earth, You who set Your glory above the heavens!" (Psalms 8:1).

"I will sing praise to Your name, O Most High" (Psalms 9:2).

"The Lord is King forever and ever" (Psalms 10:16).

"The heavens declare the glory of God" (Psalms 19:1).

"Who is the King of glory? The Lord of hosts, He is the King of glory" (Psalms 24:10).

"YOU SHALL HAVE NO OTHER GODS BEFORE ME" (Exodus 20:3).

"Therefore God also has highly exalted Him and given Him the name which is above every name, that at the name of Jesus every knee

should bow, of those in heaven, and of those on earth, and of those under the earth, and that every tongue should confess that Jesus Christ is Lord, to the glory of God the Father" (Philippians 2:9-11).

In this book God and Jesus are exalted high above everything and everyone. No one is to receive any glory except *"He who glories, let him glory in the Lord"* (II Corinthians 10:17).

"But God, who is rich in mercy, because of His great love with which He loved us, even when we were dead in trespasses, made us alive together with Christ (by grace you have been saved), and raised us up together, and made us sit together in the heavenly places in Christ Jesus, that in the ages to come He might show the exceeding riches of His grace in His kindness toward us in Christ Jesus.

For by grace you have been saved through faith, and that not of yourselves; it is the gift of God, not of works, lest anyone should boast. For we are His workmanship, created in Christ Jesus for good works, which God prepared beforehand that we should walk in them" (Ephesians 2:4-10).

We are going to be sharing some of the awesome miracles we have seen God do through us, and we want you to know from the very start that God gets all the glory and praise through Jesus. We are his workmanship, and so are you who serve Him in perfect obedience.

We are the servants; He is the Master. We do the earthly work; He gets all the praise and glory!

CHAPTER 2

PREPARE YE THE WAY!
By Frances

As we look at the glory that has been seen in our services in the past, and we look at the present and as we peer into the future through the Word of God, we can see that God has been preparing us for years for what we believe is happening now and will happen more in the near future.

When I became a Christian, the pastor who was responsible for my salvation told me very sincerely, "Frances, at your age, you'll never make it....." That could have been bad if he had stopped there, but he didn't. He continued and said, "Unless you come with the faith of a little child, just believing." That is the way I became a Christian, and that is the way I have stayed. I have never grown up - I still have that simple little child-like faith I had when I was saved.

I don't question God.

I don't question his methods.

I don't question his results.

I don't doubt God's ability!

I believe if it happened in the Bible it can happen today and I believe if Peter, James and John did it, that I can do it and I even believe that if Jesus did it, I can do it too because his Word says, *"Most assuredly, I say to you, he who believes in Me, the works that I do he will do also; and greater works than these he will do, because I go to My Father"* (John 14:12).

Jesus said it, so I believe it. If I didn't, I'd be disagreeing with God's Word, and I don't intend to do that!

When Jesus went so far as to say, *"Greater works than these he will do, because I go to My Father"*, it was for His earthly work and His glory that greater things would be done by us. We are not greater, nor do we have greater power or ability. It is simply His ability to do greater things through us than He did while He was on earth.

"And this gospel of the kingdom will be preached IN ALL THE WORLD as a witness TO ALL THE NATIONS, and then the end will come" (Matthew 24:14).

"Go therefore and make disciples of all the nations..." (Matthew 28:19).

Shortly after Charles and I were married, we were scheduled to speak at a Women's Retreat in the State of Washington. We were staying at a home on the Columbia River directly across from where the Women's Retreat was being held. There was no bridge across the river at that point, so we had to drive up twenty-five miles to the bridge, cross over, and then come back twenty-five miles to the retreat.

Sitting there eating breakfast, we were watching

the river race down to the ocean, and for a brief moment I stepped over into the supernatural world and listen to what I said to Charles because of simple, child-like faith: "Honey, why don't we just walk on the water across the river? I think that would be so neat! And we wouldn't have to drive that fifty miles today."

Then I returned to the natural world, and watch what happened as doubt and unbelief came in! I looked at Charles and said, "Maybe we'd better go in the car because we've got to take our books with us, and we probably couldn't walk on the water with the books!"

Charles and I went in the car, but today we realize that God was sowing seeds into our minds for a future time of harvest!

As we were meditating on the scripture about doing "greater" things than Jesus did, we wondered what would be greater than he did.

Charles said, "What would be greater than raising the dead? What would be greater than supernaturally feeding the multitudes? What would be greater than walking on the water? What would be greater than healing the sick?" We have been meditating on that scripture because we know that God is going to reveal something extremely significant to us through this.

Charles said, "What would be greater than raising the dead? - Raising thousands from the dead!"

"What would be greater than walking on the water like Jesus did on the Sea of Galilee? Would it be walking across the Atlantic Ocean at a supernatural speed?"

Charles continued, "What would be greater than feeding 5,000 men plus women and children? Would it be feeding 50,000 or 500,000?

Groping for a clue, he added, "Would it be translating instead of traveling on the regular airlines, ministering to the multitudes in their own languages, feeding a whole city or nation at one time, healing ALL of the sick, and then returning home the same afternoon or night so we wouldn't need a change of clothes?"

Could this be what Jesus was talking about when He said we would do greater things than He did?

We are the last Church! Peter, Paul, John, and others were in the first Church, and greater things are going to happen in these next few years until Jesus comes back than happened in the first Church.

Jesus was supernaturally feeding the people, they were walking on the water, they were translating, He turned water into wine, and so it is in the end time that just before Jesus comes back, we are going to see greater power displayed than ever before. The devil is going to come in doing supernatural miracles in greater dimensions, and those who are called to be the Peters, Pauls, and Johns of this last generation are going to be doing even greater miracles.

The Word of God shows us that as we approach the end before the return of Jesus, and finally before the acts of the book of Revelation are completed, great changes will be occurring where God will be displaying his glorious power more mightily and so will Satan be doing all he can to deceive even the elect, if that is possible, by mighty miracles.

"For as by one man's disobedience many were made sinners, so also by one Man's obedience many will be made righteous. Moreover the law entered that the offense might abound. But where sin abounded, grace abounded much more" (Romans 5:19,20).

"For false christs and false prophets will arise and show great signs and wonders, so as to deceive, if possible, even the elect" (Matthew 24:24).

"Let no one deceive you by any means; for that Day will not come unless the falling away comes first, and the man of sin is revealed, the son of perdition, who opposes and exalts himself above all that is called God or that is worshiped, so that he sits as God in the temple of God, showing himself that he is God" (II Thessalonians 2:3,4).

But praise God, Satan with his great powers is nothing when he stands before Almighty God. Jesus has already conquered him.

"Having disarmed principalities and powers, He made a public spectacle of them, triumphing over them in it" (Colossians 2:15).

Jesus is the conqueror and the King of all Kings: *"Therefore God also has highly exalted Him and given Him the name which is above every name, that at the name of Jesus every knee should bow, of those in heaven, and of those on earth, and of those under the earth, and that every tongue should confess that Jesus Christ is Lord, to the glory of God the Father"* (Philippians 2:9-11).

"And when that time comes, all doing wrong will do it more and more; the vile will become more vile; good men will be better; those who are holy will continue on in greater holiness" (Revelation 22:11 TLB).

CHAPTER 3

TRANSLATIONS
By Frances

Shortly after Charles and I were married January 1, 1970, Charles had an unusual dream.

We had to be separated a lot in the beginning of our marriage because of my speaking dates, and Charles often said it was like pulling the flesh off of his arm when he had to put me on a plane.

This particular night he had what we call today a "preparation" dream because God was preparing us for what is happening today.

Often as I would be standing in the driveway, waiting for Charles to back the car out of the garage, I would say, "Honey, why don't we just translate? That would be so much simpler!" Then doubt and unbelief would come in and I would say, "But who would see to it that our luggage would get there on time if we translated?" So we would go to the airport and get on the plane.

This particular night, Charles saw us in our back

yard with our luggage ready to go on a trip, when suddenly I just lifted up and went soaring into the sky. He said I circled around the trees in the back yard, and I kept saying to him, "Come on, honey. Come on, honey!" Charles was frantically running around the yard trying to "jump" up into the air and catch me, but it didn't work.

He strained and struggled and tried to leap into the air, only to come down again. He was frustrated because here I was up in the air, and he couldn't seem to get off the ground.

Usually in our marriage, Charles is the daring one who will do something of faith long before I do, and this was amazing to me that this time I was the one saying to him, "Come on, honey, come on!"

Finally he heard God speak to him, and He said, "Quit struggling, relax; it's by faith!" Charles relaxed and stopped running around the back yard and the next thing he knew he was up in the air flying with me as we sailed off to a speaking date. But he woke up before he found out where we were going or how our luggage got there!

If it happened in the Bible, it can happen today! The Word of God tells us, *"By faith Enoch was translated..."* (Hebrews 11:5).

How was he translated?

By faith!

Whose faith was it?

It was Enoch's faith, and it is by your own faith that you, too, will do the supernatural!

Remember when Philip was ministering to the eunuch near Gaza? When his work was finished, the

Word says, *"Now when they came up out of the water, the Spirit of the Lord caught Philip away, so that the eunuch saw him no more; and he went on his way rejoicing. But Philip was found at Azotus"* (Acts 8:39, 40).

How did he get to Azotus? Did he take a plane? Did he take a bus? No, he went on "Trinity" Airlines (Father, Son, and Holy Ghost) - he translated! Will the same thing happen today?

Years ago, my luggage was translated from Dallas, Texas, to Tulsa, Oklahoma. I told the story in our book, PRAISE THE LORD ANYWAY even though several people suggested that it was too "way out" to put in a book. Here is the story as taken from that book:

The big jet set down in Tulsa, where I was met by a pastor and his wife whom I had never seen before. They had booked me into their church at the suggestion of their youth minister, so I greeted them and they welcomed me to Tulsa, and then I said, "There's no point in looking for my luggage, because I'm sure it was misdirected in Miami." But we went to check anyway, and sure enough, no luggage! We checked into the airline counter and after an hour of checking for the luggage it couldn't be found, so the airline clerk told us to go on to the pastor's house and they would call us as soon as it was located.

His "don't call us—we'll call you" sounded ominous to me concerning my luggage, so when we got out to the pastor's car, I said, "Let's pray real quick." We held hands in the car and I very simply prayed and asked God to get my luggage to Tulsa that very night. (Doesn't everybody pray for luggage?)

The pastor had told me I was to speak at a high school assembly that next day and I knew that the right kind of clothes were important to communicate to young people. So I asked God to please see that my luggage arrived in time, and then I merely thanked Him for the way he was going to do it. I didn't know how, but I just thanked Him for whichever way He was going to do it.

I often wonder what the reaction of the pastor and his wife was toward someone who prayed for suitcases to be returned. We went on to their house anyway, had a cup of coffee, and when no call had come in, the pastor finally suggested that we call the airline, which he did, and then I talked to the clerk, who said, "Well, we finally located your luggage—it was misdirected. It's locked up in Ozark Central's depot in Dallas, Texas. They don't stay open all night, but will open at eight in the morning, and we have it on the teletype to put your luggage on the nine-thirty flight in the morning, so it will be in Tulsa before eleven and will be delivered to your house by noon."

I said, "I'm sorry, but that's too late! I have to have it tonight because I'm speaking at the high school tomorrow morning and I simply must have my clothes!" He said he was sorry because there wasn't anything he could do because the airline that would bring it tomorrow was closed for the night.

I felt a little dejected and asked if I could use the washer and dryer to wash out the suit I had on, but all of a sudden I said, "Lord, I prayed in faith believing that You would get that luggage here, so I'm not going to wash out my suit, because I BELIEVE You'll answer my prayer."

Fifteen minutes later the telephone rang and the clerk said, "You'll never believe this." I said, "Oh, yes I will" (because I knew the Lord was working). And he said, "Your luggage 'accidentally' got on an American liner and is now in Tulsa and we're putting it in a cab and sending it on to you." I said, "PRAISE THE LORD!"...and he really yelled, "What did you say?" I said "Praise the Lord"—and that's exactly what I meant, because I'd like to give you a little technical information.

The fastest time jet-wise between Dallas and Tulsa is forty-five minutes, and yet fifteen minutes after I had been advised that my luggage was visibly seen locked up in Dallas, it was in Tulsa. I felt like Peter did when he got out of jail—he couldn't understand how it happened, but he believed! And so do I believe in that "old-time" religion where God does the impossible.

In that very same book, Charles shared an out-of-the-body experience he had when his first wife was dying. He shared it again in the booklet, BORN AGAIN, WHAT DO YOU MEAN?

Charles

I want to share with you a personal experience which will, I believe, make it easier to see what happens when we receive the power. Just as it is easy to understand our spirits being conceived by the Holy Spirit when the seed-life of Jesus was planted into us by God, we ought also to see how he plants power into us.

Your spirit is exactly the same size as your body! In 1969, Jesus visited me in an unusual way. I had spent over a thousand hours meditating in the Bible, searching for ways that I could please God and Christ Jesus with my life. Early that evening Jesus had spoken to me audibly and I was exuberantly, profoundly filled with the greatest joy I had ever known! I woke up in the early hours of the morning and was praising Jesus for loving me enough to speak to me personally. I was thinking how awesome it was that he would do this to one ordinary person in a city of three million people.

While I was awake praising him, another mighty miracle took place. I was lying on my back with my arms resting along my sides, looking up to God with thanks in my heart, just loving him and thanking him for speaking to me.

Suddenly I saw another body the same size and shape of mine, lying in the same position as I was, suspended in the air about eighteen inches above my body. As I observed this, I saw that the face was identical to mine. I thought, "What can this be?" and then realized that God had taken my spirit from my body and allowed me to see it, just as I would see another person, except that the spirit body was transparent. It looked like a thin cloud or fog through which you could see, but had exactly the same shape as my own body.

The "cloud" body had no more apparent life than any other cloud in the sky until suddenly my "thinker" moved from my physical body into the spirit body. I suddenly was aware that my thinking ability and my feelings had transferred from my physical body to the spirit body, and I no longer had any sense of being in the flesh. I know now that my soul for a moment had been divided from my spirit, and then had moved from my physical body into my spirit body.

A lady who was praying for me that night had said she would lift me into the light of God in prayer. In the Spirit I saw her with her hands under my back, lifting my spirit body higher into the air. At the same time, I felt waves of energy moving through my body from my feet upward to my head; the waves, like repeating waves of the sea, increased in frequency and speed and after rising higher than the hands of the lady, my spirit body moved at a tremendous speed upward through space. I saw nothing until suddenly a few seconds through space, I was stopped and I looked about. What I saw cannot be described in our human limitations, but it was a brilliant yet soft light which lit the whole "sky."

I knew I was being held in the light of Almighty God. I was thinking normally, just like I did in my earth body: I had felt the energy and movement, just as I would in my earth body.

I wished I could have stayed there forever, but in too short a time, the same dynamic energy of the Spirit of God moved me downward through space until within short seconds I felt my spirit enter back into my earthly body. At that moment I felt in body exactly like I always have, but I knew by the experience, by faith, and by the Word of God that my spirit and soul had left my body to go on an excursion to heaven.

This was God again preparing us for greater supernatural experiences He has planned for us in these last days.

Translations were not limited to Bible times. We

have heard many people tell of translation experiences in modern times. In the book, JOHN G. LAKE ADVENTURES IN GOD, (Harrison House, Tulsa, Oklahoma, Publishers), the following experience was related:

John G. Lake was in South Africa, when asked to pray for a person in the state of Iowa, 10,000 miles away. As he had the church join in prayer, he said his spirit seemed to ascend in God, and he lost all consciousness of his environment. "Suddenly, I found myself standing in that young man's home in Iowa...The man sat by a hard coal heater with a little boy about two years old on his lap...While standing behind the man's chair, I laid my hands on his head, silently praying for God to impart to him His healing virtue and make the man well--that he might bless the world and that his mother's heart might be comforted.

"There was no knowledge of my return. In a moment I was aware that I was kneeling on the church platform. I had been uttering audible prayer and the Spirit of God was resting deeply upon the people.

"Some six weeks later, word was received that the young man was quite well. His recovery had begun on the exact date that prayer was offered for him in our church 10,000 miles away."

Another experience shared in the same book relates prayer from Johannesburg, South Africa for a man's cousin in Wales, 7,000 miles across the sea. The woman was violently insane and an inmate of an asylum in Wales.

As he was praying along with the church, he relates "Suddenly, I seemed out of the body and, to my surprise, observed that I was rapidly passing over the city of Kimberley, 300 miles from Johannesburg. I was next conscious of the city of Cape Town on the seacoast, a thousand miles away. My next consciousness was of the Island of St. Helena, where Napoleon had been banished; then the Cape Verde lighthouse on the coast of Spain.

"By this time it seemed as if I were passing through the atmosphere observing everything, but moving with great lightning-like rapidity."

"I remember the passage along the coast of France, across the Bay of Biscay, into the hills of Wales. I had never been in Wales. It was new country to me; and as I passed swiftly over its hills, I said to myself, 'These are like the hills of Wyoming along the North Dakota border'."

"Suddenly, a village appeared. It was nestled in a deep valley among the hills. Next I saw a public building that I recognized instinctively as the asylum."

"On the door I observed an old-fashioned 16th-Century knocker. Its workmanship attracted my attention and this thought flashed through my spirit: 'That undoubtedly was made by one of the old smiths who manufactured armor'."

"I was inside the institution without waiting for the doors to open and present at the side of a cot on which lay a woman. Her wrists and ankles were strapped to the sides of the cot. Another strap had been passed over her legs above the knees, and a second across her breasts. These were to hold her down."

"She was wagging her head and muttering incoherently."

I laid my hands upon her and, with great intensity, commanded in the name of Jesus Christ, the Son of God, that the demon spirit possessing her be cast out and that she be healed by the power of God."

"In a moment or two, I observed a change coming over her countenance. It softened and a look of intelligence appeared. Then her eyes opened, and she smiled up in my face. I knew she was healed."

"I had no consciousness whatever of my return to South Africa. Instantly, I was aware that I was still kneeling in prayer, and I was conscious of all the surrounding environment of my church and the service."

"Three weeks passed. Then my friend who had presented the prayer request for his cousin came to me with a letter from one of his relatives, stating that an unusual thing had occurred. Their cousin, who had been confined for seven years in the asylum in Wales, had suddenly become well. They had no explanation to offer. The doctors said it was one of those unaccountable things that sometimes occur."

Philip was a deacon in the church. He could have been an usher, a greeter, a car parker; he could have washed the dishes or served tables, but he was not the head man, and yet God chose him to translate. He is never mentioned in the Bible again after that, which shows us that God is going to take the ordinary people and give them the supernatural experiences, and that it is not only going to be the pastors and evangelists. God is looking for the same kind of a person for whom He has always looked, the individual who is responsive to God, open to whatever God has for him, and always excited to respond to the call of God, and willing, whatever the price! It can be you!

CHAPTER 4

SUPERNATURAL LANGUAGES
By Frances

Several years ago as we were speaking in a west Texas town, a man from India came into a meeting wanting to be healed of a snake bite. His foot was tremendously swollen, and he had been drinking a lot of alcohol. The Spirit directed me to call him up on the stage. I asked him if he was saved, and he replied, "No." I then led him in a sinner's prayer before laying hands on him for the baptism with the Holy Spirit and healing.

He fell under the power of the Holy Spirit and began speaking in tongues, when suddenly he jumped to his feet, amazed at what had happened to the snake bite, and began to speak to me in a foreign language. He was obviously questioning me about something, so I spoke to him in tongues. He asked another question, then another, and each time I answered him in tongues. Then another question. Another answer in tongues. Another question. Another answer in tongues. This continued for ten or fifteen minutes with the entire audience basking in the glory of God because it looked like we were both speaking in tongues. He finally seemed satisfied, so he left the stage saved, baptized with the Holy Spirit, he had fallen under the power of God, and was healed!

Several years later we were back in the same town and the couple who had sponsored the meeting told us an interesting thing. They said, "Do you remember the man from India who came to that meeting with the snake bite?" We answered in the affirmative.

Then they said, "When he left the meeting he came over to us and said, 'Where did that woman learn to talk the Indian language? Not only did she speak the language, but the dialect from the country where I come from. I asked her what had happened to me on the stage because I had sobered up, and she told me about Jesus who died on the cross for the forgiveness of my sins. She said that my sins were gone because He loved me that much. She said he had sent back the Holy Spirit to give us power to live the Christian life and that was the language I had been speaking while on the floor. Then she told me that God's power had touched me personally and that was why I fell down'!"

God had supernaturally given me a language which I did not know with which to converse with this man so that he would know about the plan of salvation and exactly what had happened to him! Glory!

This again was God preparing us for future activities of the Spirit world into which he is taking the Body of Christ at an ever-increasing rate!

At the Teen Challenge Farm in Rehrersburg, Pennsylvania, Charles gave a message in tongues and I interpreted it. He said as this message came forth from his spirit that it was the most beautiful language he had ever heard. In his natural mind he was thinking, "God, this is so unusual and I am pronouncing words that are so different; I wonder what this is?"

The message was rather lengthy and so was my interpretation. We are blessed to see God using these gifts often through us in our meetings, and generally the interpretation comes as though thoughts are coming into our minds, but we can clearly distinguish our thoughts from God's.

We didn't realize what an unusual experience we were having until the next night a retired Dutch school teacher who was a language expert came to us before the meeting and said, "Charles, that was the most beautiful thing I have ever heard as you gave the message in tongues last night. You were speaking in perfect high German, even using the accent of a German doing the speaking with the perfect diction and pronounciation. It was so perfect, but then Frances gave not only the interpretation, but an actual translation of every word in perfect English!"

Neither of us know any German other than "Gesundheit!" and that's not very high German! Again God was opening our spirits in preparation for something more.

We were ministering during an evening service at the PTL Club Barn and Charles was ministering the baptism with the Holy Spirit to a group of about 150 people while I was laying hands on the sick. When we instruct Christians on how to receive the gift of the

Holy Spirit, we illustrate by speaking in tongues so they will have heard someone actually speak in the spirit language.

I Corinthians 14:2 says, *"For he who speaks in a tongue does not speak to men but to God, for no one understands him; however, in the spirit he speaks mysteries."*

Charles was talking to God with his spirit and when he finished he looked intently at one young lady in the group and thought he was illustrating speaking in tongues again. It was just a short sentence.

When they had all received the baptism with the Holy Spirit and they all spoke in tongues, the young lady came to Charles and said, "Charles, I am Jewish. It took me a long time to believe that Jesus Christ is the Messiah, but I have been born again and He is my Savior. But when you were telling us how to receive the gift of the Holy Spirit, doubt came into my mind like it had before I accepted Jesus, and I was about to give up the thought of receiving when you looked at me and in perfect Hebrew (Charles doesn't know a word of Hebrew) you said, 'Relax and it will come easily!' "

As soon as Charles said that to her, she lifted her hands and began speaking in other tongues as the Spirit gave the utterance, her new language of the Spirit. God had given one of his chosen children a sign and wonder so she would believe.

"Now when the Day of Pentecost had fully come, they were all with one accord in one place. And suddenly there came a sound from heaven, as of a rushing mighty wind, and it filled the whole house where they were sitting. Then there appeared to them divided

tongues, as of fire, and one sat upon each of them. And they were all filled with the Holy Spirit and BEGAN TO SPEAK WITH OTHER TONGUES, as the Spirit gave them utterance."

"Now there were dwelling in Jerusalem Jews, devout men, from every nation under heaven. And when this sound occurred, the multitude came together, and were confused, because EVERYONE HEARD THEM SPEAK IN HIS OWN LANGUAGE. Then they were all amazed and marveled, saying to one another, 'Look, are not all these who speak Galileans? And how is it that we hear, each in our own language in which we were born? Parthians and Medes and Elamites, those dwelling in Mesopotamia, Judea and Cappadocia, Pontus and Asia, Phrygia and Pamphylia, Egypt and the parts of Libya adjoining Cyrene, visitors from Rome, both Jews and proselytes, Cretans and Arabs--WE HEAR THEM SPEAKING IN OUR OWN TONGUES THE WONDERFUL WORKS OF GOD' " (Acts 2:1-11).

Peter declared after this wonderful miracle of God that this was what had been spoken by the prophet Joel. We are a part of that great and mighty wind of the Holy Spirit that is still blowing full force and will continue until Jesus returns for us! Glory!

Speaking in languages we don't know so that people who know those languages will understand and see the glory of God is happening today all over the world. We hear of many such incidents and we have spoken in perhaps eight or ten languages which we have been told were recognized: Korean, Hawaiian, an almost extinct Chinese language, Greek, Hebrew, Indian and who knows what else.

One night a Christian lady brought her non-Christian husband to one of our meetings. That night one of us gave a message in tongues and Charles interpreted it. This lady called us the next day to tell what her husband said. He asked her why we said something and then turned right around and said it again! Glory to God, he had heard an utterance of the wonderful works of God both in tongues and in English and didn't know the difference. Hallelujah!

God is confirming in so many ways by sowing seeds as we progress in his service for the end-time harvest of souls.

CHAPTER 5

SHIFTING GEARS
By Charles

In August, 1982, we were traveling in Michigan and listening to a cassette tape on the way to our next meeting. The speaker was talking about Peter walking on the water.

As he told this story, a truth from God exploded in my spirit and I exclaimed, "Frances, did you hear what I just heard?"

I had always presumed that when Peter saw Jesus walking on the water there was a supernatural power because Jesus was there, and had He not been there, Peter would not have been able to do this remarkable miracle.

The speaker continued on to say that Peter did not walk on the water in the flesh, but in the Spirit. Regardless of his desires, he would have sunk had he been walking in the fleshly realm.

He referred to the scripture which says, *"For what the law could not do in that it was weak through the flesh, God did by sending His own Son in the likeness of sinful flesh, on account of sin: He condemned sin in the flesh, that the righteous requirement of the law might be fulfilled in us WHO DO NOT WALK AC-CORDING TO THE FLESH BUT ACCORDING TO THE SPIRIT. For those who live according to the flesh set their minds on the things of the flesh, but those who live according to the Spirit, the things of the Spirit''* (Romans 8:3-5).

In a burst of spirit revelation, I saw that it was Peter, the ordinary fisherman, who made the decision to walk to Jesus. Peter the man made up his own mind! It was not Jesus forcing him to walk on the water. It was not because Jesus was giving off some extra power from God, but it was Peter himself who stepped forth into a supernatural realm by simply exercising his faith in Jesus. He decided and then acted on his decision.

Peter moved from the sense realm of the flesh into the supernatural realm of the Spirit - by faith! It was as though he shifted gears and moved into another world!

I said, "Frances, if Peter did it, we can do it, too! If it is in the Bible, we can do anything that they did because Jesus said, " *'Most assuredly, I say to you, he who believes in Me, the works that I do he will do also; and greater works than these he will do, because I go to My Father. And whatever you ask in My name, that I will do, that the Father may be glorified in the Son. If you ask anything in My name, I will do it'* " (John 14:12-14).

Peter had just said to Jesus, *"Lord, if it is You, command me to come to You on the water"* (Matthew 14:28).

It is important to remember that anything and

everything we do in the supernatural must be done to fulfill God's purposes and not our own. The desire of Peter's heart was to go to Jesus. He was afraid of the storm and he was frightened because he thought he had just seen a ghost. I doubt that he was thinking about doing a miracle of walking on water; he was thinking about getting to the one who could save him from the storm. Pride can destroy us, but pride will never come in doing the supernatural if we will always fix our minds on God.

God opened a new dimension of His glory to us that day in the twinkling of an eye!

We have taught HOW TO HEAL THE SICK for years to tens of thousands of people and we constantly tell them, "If Charles and Frances can do it, you can do it, too! If Jesus did it while He was on the earth, you can do it, too, because He said we could do the same things He did and even greater things."

I said, "Frances, we have been shifting gears from the fleshly realm to a dimension of the Spirit realm for years. When we operate in the gift of word of knowledge for healings, we do it because God speaks to us, but we decide ourselves at which moment to shift into the supernatural realm of the Spirit and speak it out."

Jesus commands us in the Great Commission to do the preaching, casting out devils, speaking in tongues, and healing the sick. The scriptures tell us that we are the Body of Christ who have been given the responsibility to do miracles for Him.

If Jesus commands us to do something, He certainly will give us the power and ability to do it.

Then we thought, "If we shift gears to perform miracles of healing, what else can we shift gears to do in the supernatural realm?"

We began to talk to each other about different things God had done through us which would fall in the category of walking in the Spirit and not in the flesh.

We thought, "We can give a message in tongues and interpretation any time we feel led of the Spirit to do so. We are the ones who step into the supernatural to do it. We are the ones who shift gears from the natural to the supernatural.

"We lay hands on people and they fall under the power of God. That's in the supernatural Spirit realm, so we have been shifting gears to move into that dimension."

"We have had visions while operating in the word of knowledge for inner healings. God gives the visions, but we move into that dimension by our will TO DO HIS WILL."

Then we thought, "We haven't walked on physical water like Jesus and Peter did - YET! But if Peter could do it we can do it. God, we are ready to walk on water, so give us the opportunity and we will step out in faith for You!"

We began meditating on the full meaning of this mighty truth, new to us but given to us long ago by Jesus! We began to reflect on the things He has done in our lives which are mighty and glorify God and Christ Jesus. We began sharing parts of this new revelation in our meetings, and saw the response of the people. It seemed to bring new hope, new faith to them as they caught the vision of what God wants to do through his people in this age.

As we have asked congregation after congregation how many of them believe that we are in the very last generation before the return of Jesus, they seem to unanimously and spontaneously all lift their hands excitedly.

One day I said to Frances, "Do you realize that God has let us live in this last generation? Do you also realize that the Bible indicates that the miracles and wonders of God will be greater in the end generation than in the first generation of the church? The devil will do mighty miracles in the end times, but God will do greater miracles.

"Frances, somebody will be the Peters, James, Johns and Pauls of this generation, and we are going to be among that team of disciples!"

Frances said, "I'll be a Pauline!"

That began to reach down into our spirits so strongly that we began to feel the awesome responsibility God is giving to those of us in this last generation who will lay down our lives for Jesus and be willing to give all to do his works, his miracles, on earth to win the multitudes to the kingdom of God! WE ARE THE BODY OF CHRIST, AND WE ARE THE DISCIPLES CHOSEN BY JESUS FOR THIS LAST GENERATION. WHAT ARE WE GOING TO DO ABOUT IT?

Paul counted the cost to be a disciple. Stephen counted the cost. Every great man of faith counted the cost. All those who were counted worthy to be disciples counted the cost but were willing to do anything to follow Jesus.

"Then Peter began to say to Him, 'See, we have left all and followed You.'

"So Jesus answered and said, 'Assuredly, I say to you, there is no one who has left house or brothers or sisters or father or mother or wife or children or lands, for My sake and the gospel's, who shall not receive a hundredfold now in this time - houses and brothers and sisters and mothers and children and lands, with persecutions - and in the age to come, eternal life. But many who are first will be last, and the last first' (Mark 10:28-31)."

Some people are willing to go all the way with Jesus to gain all the world, but not to receive the gain with persecutions. Some people are willing to go all the way at any cost.

Paul said to Timothy, *"Yes, and all who desire to live godly in Christ Jesus will suffer persecution"* (II Timothy 3:12).

Jesus Himself said, *"If the world hates you, you know that it hated Me before it hated you. If you were of the world, the world would love its own. Yet because you are not of the world, but I chose you out of the world, therefore the world hates you. Remember the word that I said to you, 'A servant is not greater than his master.' If they persecuted Me, they will also persecute you. If they kept My word, they will keep yours also"* (John 15:18-20).

We don't want to think of persecution any more than you do, but since Jesus said that was going to be a part of serving Him, we are willing to do whatever He wants because we love Him more than even our lives.

Will it be worth the cost?

"But what things were gain to me, these I have counted loss for Christ. But indeed I also count all things loss for the excellence of the knowledge of Christ Jesus my Lord, for whom I have suffered the loss of all things, and count them as rubbish, that I may gain Christ and be found in Him, not having my own righteousness, which is from the law, but that which is through faith in Christ, the righteousness which is from God by faith; that I may know Him and the power of His resurrection, and the fellowship of His sufferings, being conformed to His death, if, by any means, I may attain to the resurrection from the dead" (Philippians 3:7-11).

Frances and I are going to be a part of it! Are you?

CHAPTER 6

THEN AND NOW
By Charles

We are reflecting on some of the greatest miracles we have seen in our ministry, and the wide variety of miracles. We began to recall similar types of miracles God said would happen, and which did happen in the Bible.

We began to realize more and more that everything God has done in the Bible will be repeated in similar ways in this final chapter of time before Jesus returns to gather up his Church and whisk us away to introduce us personally in our glorified bodies to our glorious Father. What a day that will be, and it isn't far away! GLORY!

Soon after we had received the gift of the Holy Spirit, and God began to do miracles through us just as he had done through Jesus and His disciples, I was reading in the Living Bible and saw something that was a thrill to me. About ten o'clock that morning I called Frances from my CPA office and said, "Sweetheart, we are going to see new arms and legs grow on people who have had them cut off; like a person with a peg leg growing a new one!"

The scripture I had read that morning was, *"And a vast crowd brought him their lame, blind, maimed, and those who couldn't speak, and many others, and laid them before Jesus, and he healed them all. What a spectacle it was! Those who hadn't been able to say a word before were talking excitedly, and those with missing arms and legs had new ones; the crippled were walking and jumping around, and those who had been blind were gazing about them! The crowds just marveled, and praised the God of Israel"* (Matthew 15:30, 31 TLB).

About two weeks later we went to a church in West Palm Beach, Florida. The pastor had told us that we must be out of the church by nine o'clock because his people would walk out if we kept them too late. About eleven o'clock the whole audience was standing, some on the floor, some on the seats, and some even standing on top of the back of the pews holding on to those in front of them.

God was displaying His glory that night with mighty signs and wonders and miracles!

A boy about fourteen years old came to the altar. The glory of God was shining all over him and he was crying with joy he couldn't contain.

We asked, "What would you like for Jesus to do for you?"

He stuck out his left hand and said, "Grow me a

new thumb.''

His thumb had been cut off when he was four years old. It was a peculiar-looking amputation, because it looked like the skin had been pulled together and tied, rather than left smooth.

GLORY TO GOD! THIS WAS OUR FIRST OP-PORTUNITY TO SEE A CUT-OFF LIMB GROW BACK!

We said, "Stick out your hands!" He did. We commanded it to grow and nothing happened. Frances said, "Put out both arms and hold them together."

He stretched forth both arms, side by side, so we could watch both arms and thumbs at the same time.

Again we commanded, "Grow, thumb, grow, in Jesus' name!"

In fact, we yelled at the thumb. Our faith was high, because we had just read in the Bible that this had happened with the disciples of the early church.

Suddenly, with the whole audience standing, watching to see what the power of God would do, the thumb stub began to grow. Slowly, slowly it moved forward!

It grew right out to full size, just like the other thumb!

The audience went wild with excitement! Just like we had read in the Bible, *"The crowds just marveled, and praised the God of Israel!"*

GLORY TO OUR MIGHTY GOD!''

If it happened in the Bible, it should happen again today, and it did! Hallelujah!

We will see cut-off arms and legs grow just that way in this generation!

CHAPTER 7

VISIONS AND DREAMS
By Charles

"And it shall come to pass afterward that I will pour out My Spirit on all flesh; your sons and your daughters shall prophesy, your old men shall dream dreams, your young men shall see visions; and also on My menservants and on My maidservants I will pour out My Spirit in those days" (Joel 2:28).

If God promised we would dream dreams and see visions, we WILL dream spiritual dreams and see spiritual visions because we are in the days God said this would happen.

Just prior to receiving the baptism with the Holy Spirit, we went to a Kathryn Kuhlman miracle service in Pittsburgh, Pennsylvania. This was our first exposure to the great present-day miracle power of God. Each of us had been divinely healed and we had seen a few miracles, but that morning we saw multitudes healed!

Something else really made an impression on us. This lady stood before an audience and pointed to dif-

ferent parts of the church and said, "A man over there
has just been healed of a leg problem. He is wearing a
brace on his left leg. Take off the brace and come
here!"

Sure enough, right where she pointed, a man took
off his brace from his left leg and walked normally.
What an awesome spectacle that was.

She said, "There is a little girl right back there
who had cancer with big lumps all over her body. God
just healed you, honey. Come here!"

We had stood outside in a vast crowd before the
service waiting and hoping to get in. This little girl was
right next to us, held in her daddy's arms. She was gray
and looked like death was near. Lumps the size of eggs
or even larger were all over that child's body. We had
said, "God, if it is a choice of her or us getting in, let
her get in to get healed."

Suddenly we saw this same little girl, now healthy,
pink and robust, running down the aisle without spot
or wrinkle - free of the curse of the devil who had put
those lumps all over her body.

Afterwards we talked with each other, wondering
how Kathryn Kuhlman knew about these healings in
the audience. We knew it was supernatural. We knew
God had to someway tell her about it. We knew that if
someone else could do it, it was possible for us to do it.
But how could this be?

Soon afterwards we accepted the great gift of the
Holy Spirit and spoke in tongues just like on the Day
of Pentecost, and sure enough we received an enduement of power just like they did. This is one of the
greatest signs and wonders of all in the Bible. That

God, even the God of Israel, would fill us with his own mighty power, and he had, and we were seeing an increase almost daily in the miracles done by this new-found, heaven-sent power, all in the wonderful name of Jesus!

We kept asking God, "How did she know about these miracles in the audience." We believed that if we would ask God, he would tell us, and sure enough, it wasn't but a few months before he did.

Even before Frances was born again by the Spirit of God, she had experienced a mighty vision. To my knowledge, I had never experienced one.

One night, Frances was speaking to an audience in Houston, Texas, when suddenly she pointed way back toward the back of the church and said, "That man who is sitting about five rows from the back on the aisle, you have just been healed of an ulcer. Come here, please."

Then she pointed to four others, describing what they had, and telling them they had been healed.

All five of these came forward and testified of being healed exactly as Frances had said.

As soon as we were alone, I said, "How did you do that!"

I knew that she had shifted gears and moved into a new dimension for us. I wanted to know how, so I could be a part of what God was doing.

Frances said she had seen each of the five in a vision. It was just as plain as looking with the eyes, but it was seeing in the Spirit realm, in a vision, instead of with the natural eyes.

Joel's words from God were being made alive in

the twentieth century. Frances had entered into a dimension of the Spirit realm just as God had promised long ago that would happen in these last days.

We talked about this and marveled that God had revealed to her a way of walking not after the flesh, but "after the Spirit."

We are in the world, but not of the world. (See John 15:19).

Frances had walked not after the flesh, but after the Spirit.

Peter had found the entrance into this Spirit world when he walked on water. Frances found a way to walk through that door into a new dimension.

I knew that if Frances had found the secret of transferring from one world into another, I could learn from her how to do it.

We realized early in our relationship with God that the supernatural could be learned and taught. We were looking for the keys that would unlock the doors into this supernatural world.

Frances had found one of the keys, revealed to her by the Spirit. It was quite awhile before we knew that this was called the gift of the word of knowledge in I Corinthians 12:8.

Shortly after that I learned from the Spirit how to operate in the gift of word of knowledge and call out healings and describe them. God revealed that gift to me in a totally different way. I could sense a presence much like a magnetic field in a particular place in the audience. I had sincerely asked God to tell me how to do that, and I expected Him to tell me. If you will believe, you will see the glory of God!

By faith that God had made this magnetic field appear in the audience, I pointed to the place where it was, and said, "Someone right over there has been healed." Sure enough someone right in the middle of that area rose to testify that they had just been healed by the power of God.

Frances got me aside real quickly, and said, "How did you do that?"

I explained how I had been letting my mind float over the audience as I prayed for them and her while she was speaking, when I sensed this force field of energy in a certain area and believed God had made this appear so that I would know where his glory was being poured out.

We both began to expect this field of energy, this magnetic field, to appear, and sure enough, God let us both find the healings in the audience this way for quite awhile.

One night I was opening my spirit to find a field of energy. (I think of it like an area where it is raining off in the distance in one spot and you can see the whole rain area). A spot in the audience came to me where the energy field was located, and I said in my thoughts, "God, Kathryn Kuhlman knew what was being healed as well as where it was located. How did she do that?"

Years before I had discovered that I could think to God, and He would "think" back to me. I did this by relaxing my mind when I would think a question or thought to Him, and a thought would come into my mind. I knew that if I thought, it took a certain effort on my part, but when the thought came from God, it came without any effort. I learned to distinguish His thoughts from my thoughts.

When I asked God how Kathryn Kuhlman identified what was being healed, I simply relaxed my body (after I found my "rainstorm" in the audience) and felt a sharp pain in my left elbow. I thought, "God, are you telling me that someone in that little energy area has an elbow problem which you are healing?"

So by faith that God had spoken, I pointed to the energy field and said, "Someone right over there has a pain in your elbow. God just healed you, so stand up and tell us what happened."

A lady quickly stood to her feet and said she had this elbow problem and had pain just as I said, but that the pain left and she was healed.

Again Frances grabbed me and said, "How did you do that?"

After telling her how I moved through the door from the natural man into the Spirit realm, we both operated in the gift of word of knowledge in this manner, and still do. I almost always use this method of hearing God for a word of knowledge for healings, but Frances uses other methods as well to effectively identify the healings in the audience. We know by faith and by actual experience that a word of knowledge from God by His Holy Spirit is always accurate.

You might be interested in knowing that God stopped letting us see the energy field not long after he started showing that. We believe the reason is that we were limited to one person at a time being healed and many times we call out a healing and many people are healed at one time. God is bringing back his Glory!

Visions are being given to God's people in this day

just as he said they would be.

Peter saw a vision when God showed him the sheet coming down from above with the unclean things on it, telling Peter that he wanted him to go to the gentiles with the good news that Jesus is the Messiah! Peter saw the vision three times, but still he thought about it for perhaps three days before he really understood what God meant by this.

Many visions were described as happening in the Bible, and this is simply God opening our spirit minds to let us see what He wants us to see.

If visions happened to the disciples, then we can expect visions to happen to us disciples of this end generation. And what happens when we expect God to do something? He does it.

Frances and I have experienced many visions, she more than I.

One day we were operating in the word of knowledge gift in healing when I saw in the Spirit a human brain without a skull over it. It appeared to have a light inside it to make all the little grooves in the brain show up plainly.

It was as though I was standing over this brain, and I began searching for what God was showing me. It was beautifully perfect, without a flaw or mark, except for a tiny spot about the size of a small fingernail where there appeared to be a little scab or something similar.

God had shown me something through a vision which was afflicting someone in our audience. I described this vision as best I could and told of the tiny spot and said it appeared to me to be a tumor.

A lady came forward, telling us that the doctors had discovered a brain tumor and that when I called it out, the pain left her instantly! I put my finger where I had seen the spot in my spirit, and she said I had my finger on the exact spot! Glory to God, what a divine X-ray God uses when He gives us a vision.

That is by the Spirit of God - not by our flesh. It is a vision, not an imagination.

Beware and be careful if you are one whom God chooses to do his work through visions. Imagination is so similar to visions that many get in the flesh and think God is giving a vision. You can become sensitive to the Holy Spirit, and if you are not walking after the flesh to glorify self, you will be able to recognize the voice of the Master, instead of being in the flesh with imagination.

On another occasion we were operating in the word of knowledge to go back in time for healings necessary because people hold on to memories of traumatic experiences and allow the devil to molest their minds. They vitally need teaching on how to recognize that your old self is dead when you are born again, and you become a new creature, free from the bondage of the past.

When the woman at the well talked with Jesus, He told her about her past. He, by the gifts of the Spirit of God, moved back in time to tell her that she was living with a man who was not her husband, but that she had been married five times before (John 4:17).

Jesus changed the lives of most of the people in her village when she believed that Jesus was the Messiah because He knew things about her which He had no fleshly way to know. God gives us these gifts to do His work, and Jesus had added another group of souls to His Father's riches by the working of miracles and signs and wonders. He had shifted gears to move from the flesh realm into the Spirit realm.

One day Frances was given a vision by God in one of our services. In her spirit realm she saw a little girl about five years old, in a field of wheat which was taller than she, alone and frightened. She was running at breakneck speed because she was so afraid.

Frances said, "There is a person in this audience who once was lost in a field, alone and frightened. You were wearing a yellow polka dot dress, and because of that experience, you have had fear in your life ever since!"

This girl, now nearing thirty years of age, came to Frances with this story. She said, "I remember it vividly. You described perfectly what happened to me and it was like you had a color photograph of the entire scene." She had gone through about twenty-five years of her life possessed by fear and had become a nervous wreck. She had other accompanying illnesses caused by the fear instilled in her memory long before.

Because she knew that God had recognized her need and told Frances about it, her faith rose and she was set free!

Notice as we share experiences of things happening in this generation which happened in the Bible, that each time God is doing His work in lives through the Spirit realm, and that it is never for the glory of mankind.

One of the most fantastic events we have ever seen

was shared in our book, IMPOSSIBLE MIRACLES. The following is an excerpt from that book:

Frances: **A VISION IS A MIRACLE!**

"His glory covered the heavens,
And the earth was full of His praise.
His brightness was like the light;
HE HAD RAYS FLASHING FROM HIS HAND"
(Habakkuk 3:3, 4).

The final night of a Delightfully Charismatic Christian Walk Seminar in Calgary, Canada, was a night of power like we've never seen in our entire ministry.

Faith was at top level because of the seminar teachings. That night's subject was marriage, and as Charles was talking about honesty in marriage, I felt such a tremendous wave of power I nearly fell over. I grabbed the podium and looked over at Charles to see if he felt the same thing I did.

I couldn't believe my eyes!

Out of the ends of his fingers were shooting flames of blue fire about four inches long, and as I looked at them, God spoke to me and said, "The healing anointing is upon Charles. The first thirty people who reach the altar will be instantly healed!"

I had to interrupt Charles! The power was increasing to such an extent I knew God had something special! I repeated to the audience what God had said, and it looked like the entire auditorium turned upside-down. I never saw sick and crippled people move so fast in my entire life!

As Charles ran off the stage to lay hands on them, the power of God was so strong they fell in waves as he ran through the crowd. When he was about half-way across the front of the auditorium, he raised his hands to touch some, and about thirty to forty people fell under the power at the same time. People began weeping all over the auditorium as they felt the power of God in a way they had never felt it before.

Bob and Joan were offstage at this particular moment, but they felt something supernatural come through even the loudspeaker. Bob said, "I heard Frances say, 'Get out of the way and let Charles through,' then I heard the word 'fire!' I came running out as fast as I could, wondering if there had been a bomb of some kind or other. There was - A HOLY GHOST BOMB! Charles was plowing through the crowd and people were falling all over the place!"

Joan said, "I kept hearing 'let him through, let him through, there's fire on his hands,' so I ran to the curtain at the back of the stage. The power of God was so strong it felt exactly like a solid wall of God's beautiful power, and I broke into tears, completely overcome by the overwhelming presence of God."

By this time Charles had gone almost across the auditorium, and the flames began to diminish, and finally they disappeared. He came back up onto the stage, and asked the people to raise their hands if the KNEW they were healed. More than 100 hands were raised, as God gave even more than he had promised.

It is impossible to explain how you feel in a moment like this. I was so awed by what I had seen and heard that I just stood there wondering what was going to happen next!

I didn't have to wait but just a few seconds and then I saw things I had never seen in my entire life. The Jubilee Auditorium is a large auditorium with two balconies, and an extremely high ceiling. As I looked out over the people, there appeared a huge dove with a wingspread of about fifty feet hovering on the left-hand side of the auditorium.

It was not white!

Instead, it was "like as of fire."

The dove looked exactly as if it had been carved right out of fire! It was red, orange and yellow!

I have never felt the awesome presence of God as I did at that moment, then a shocking thing began to happen!

The quills from the wings of the dove began flying out across the audience and landing on various people.

It looked like skyrockets exploding as the quills flew faster and faster across the auditorium.

God spoke again and said, "There is perversion in the sexual life of married couples here. There is adultery in marriages here, and I am sending the fire of my Holy Spirit to burn it out."

Men and women began weeping as they cried out, "God save me!"

The presence of God was a reality to many people who had never before felt his presence.

The convicting power of the Holy Spirit was upon many marriages...then...

As suddenly as it had appeared, the dove disappeared!

It was instantly replaced by a white dove.

I told the audience the dove "like as of fire" had disappeared and had been replaced by a white one, and waited for another message from God because I didn't understand this at all.

God gave Charles the message this time and he said, "I have sent my white dove as a symbol of purification. Your marriages have been cleansed and purified. Keep them that way!"

The white dove was gone!

Hundreds of people accepted Jesus as a result of this awe-inspiring moment and many were baptized in the Holy Spirit and healed at the same time. It was estimated that around 1,800 people fell under the power of God this one night.

We may never again stand in the Shekinah glory of God until we get to heaven, but our lives will never be the same again as a result of this night.

Some people might not believe it; maybe you won't, but we have to, because we were there!

An IMPOSSIBLE MIRACLE, but it happened!

What else was there to be done that night? We went back to the stage and simply said, "That's all God wants to do tonight" and dismissed the audience. We slipped back of the stage curtain but one young lady made her way to us and was so excited she could hardly speak. She said, "My father has committed sexual intercourse with every member of our family, male and female, children, nephews and nieces, uncles and aunts. He was the first one who screamed out, 'God save me!' He fell under the power of God and started speaking in other tongues as he received the baptism with the Holy Spirit!"

In Psalm 7:11-17 TLB we found an interesting confirmation of the flaming quills: *"God is a judge who is perfectly fair, and he is angry with the wicked every day. Unless they repent, he will sharpen his sword and slay them. He has bent and strung his bow and FITTED IT WITH DEADLY ARROWS MADE FROM SHAFTS OF FIRE. The wicked man conceives an evil plot, labors with its dark details, and brings to birth his treachery and lies; let him fall into his own trap. May the violence he plans for others boomerang upon himself; let him die. Oh, how grateful and thankful I am to the Lord because he is so good. I will sing praise to the name of the Lord who is above all lords."*

Charles:

God frequently communicated with His prophets or others by dreams as well as visions.

Dreams and visions are defined as being alike, except that one comes while you are awake and the other while you are asleep.

Webster's dictionary says a vision means "to see in or as in a vision; to dream." Another definition given is "something seen, especially something such as might be seen in a dream or trance." A further definition of a vision is "that which is supposedly seen by other than normal sight; a supernatural, prophetic, or imaginary appearance; something seen in a dream...".

It is important in anything of the supernatural to be sold out to God and seasoned well in his Word so that we will not be misled. As humans we use our minds to think or reason, but sometimes we use them to imagine things which are not real.

Imaginations and visions are similar and unless we are wanting to do what God says to do, we can be misled in thinking we are seeing a vision when it is nothing more than our imagination.

How can we sort out the visions, dreams, thoughts, imaginations, and daydreams to determine what is of God, what is of the devil, or what is our own thinking or imagination?

Always examine a vision, dream, or imaginative thought to see if it lines up with the Word of God. Does it point toward God, others, or toward self? Is the person telling of the visions or dreams living a holy life and meditating in the Bible to please God, or to please self. Jesus must be exalted at all times.

Be very sensitive to the Holy Spirit, but it is always a good idea to be cautious about acting upon a dream or vision. Make certain that God is the communicator of a message to us. He will always make it clear if our hearts are in tune with His Spirit and His Word.

We personally have heard from God much more in visions (daytime, awake) than in dreams.

Daydreaming and meditating are closely related and both can be a means of hearing from God. I can now credit to God a daydream I had long ago. When I was about twenty-five years old, right after I became a Certified Public Accountant, I was pondering over my future desires - I was daydreaming.

I was in the United States Air Force, stationed in England. I was thinking about my future and thought, "When I get out of military service, I will either work for a major oil company and make my way to an executive position, or I will go to work with a large CPA firm and eventually become a partner, or I will go into an accounting practice of my own." I had previously talked with a Christian man who was a CPA and we discussed the possibility of going into practice together, but it seemed a passing thought. Within a week after I left the Air Force, I was in partnership with this fellow Christian.

Little did I realize then that God would speak to me in this manner, but I know now that He was directing my thoughts to be in an independent position that He would use for His purposes in the future. Frances and I can see clearly the many uses God made of the experiences in my training, and the positions He has placed us in for His divine direction. God directs our paths if we WANT to do what He wants us to do. Even way back then, I wanted to follow Jesus my whole life. You can be drawn into God's purpose if your whole desire is to please Him, but if you have selfish desires, you will pull away from His plans for your life.

Another daydream God used was also in His plans for me to be a CPA. Before I entered my first partnership with the Christian I mentioned above, I "thought" (daydreamed), "I will work hard until I am fifty-five years old, and then I will half retire so I can use a lot of time for my own pleasure." I even thought I would live near a lake so I could learn to enjoy fishing and even purchased a lot on a hill overlooking a beautiful lake.

All of my agreements and plans with partners throughout my career were made in such a way that I could be free when I was fifty-five.

But God had His plans working in my life and used what I thought were my plans for His purposes. God clearly, supernaturally spoke to me that Frances and I would be in a joint ministry.

Guess what happened when I was fifty-five years old! In 1969 God spoke to me and told me to cut down on my practice fifty percent. He didn't say when; He just said to do it. We were married in 1970. Frances was an evangelist and was traveling most of the time and I was still in my CPA practice. I went with her as often as I could, and at the end of that year discovered from our computer records that I had worked half time; I had half retired, not for my desires but for God's work. An error in MY thinking was that God brought me to half time when I was fifty instead of fifty-five. I was fully retired from my CPA practice and was in full-time service for God when I reached fifty-five. He was directing my desires all along and I thought I was doing it! Hallelujah!

God is a great God, and I know that He can give us daydreams which are supernatural although they seem just natural to us.

So that we can all be alert to God's communication through dreams and visions, we want you to look at some of the ways God talked with His people in the Bible.

Joseph was an interpreter of dreams. Pharaoh had dreamed and tried to get the magicians of Egypt to tell him the meaning. They failed to do it, but someone told him that Joseph could interpret it for him. *"Then Pharaoh sent and called Joseph, and they brought him hastily out of the dungeon; and he shaved, changed his clothing, and came to Pharaoh. And Pharaoh said to Joseph, 'I have dreamed a dream, and there is no one who can interpret it. But I have heard it said of you that you can understand a dream, to interpret it.' So Joseph answered Pharaoh, saying, 'It is not in me; God will give Pharaoh an answer of peace' "* (Genesis 41:14-16).

The devil is limited in his abilities but does have just enough of the supernatural to confuse us if we don't really know God is speaking. We must stay in the Word of God until it is written upon our hearts and minds, and we will know, like Joseph did, that it is not in us; God will give us the answer of peace.

Now look at how the devil can imitate God; learn to recognize the difference. *"If there arises among you a prophet or a dreamer of dreams, and he gives you a sign or a wonder, and the sign or the wonder of which he spoke to you comes to pass, saying, 'Let us go after other gods which you have not known, and let us serve them,' you shall not listen to the words of that prophet or that dreamer of dreams, for the Lord your God is testing you to know whether you love the Lord your God with all your heart and with all your soul. You shall walk after the Lord your God and fear Him, and keep His commandments and obey His voice, and you shall serve Him and hold fast to Him.*

"But that prophet or that dreamer of dreams shall be put to death, because he has spoken in order to turn you away from the Lord your God, who brought you out of the land of Egypt and redeemed you from the house of bondage, to entice you from the way in which

the Lord your God commanded you to walk. So you shall put away the evil from your midst" (Deuteronomy 13:1-5).

Many people who don't really know God's Word and who don't live a holy life before God, will give "a word from the Lord" which may be sincere, but which is selfish in its nature and purpose. It is through such false prophets today that the devil tries to get us to SERVE ANOTHER GOD (self), rather than the Almighty God. BEWARE!

If God actually put such a person to death today, these misleading false prophets would be afraid to utter careless words in the name of God. Actually, they are dead in the spirit.

And yet God wants to speak to His people in this generation, so LISTEN! Jesus said, *"My sheep hear My voice, and I know them, and they follow Me"* (John 10:27). *"Most assuredly, I say to you, he who does not enter the sheepfold by the door, but climbs up some other way, the same is a thief and a robber. But he who enters by the door is the shepherd of the sheep. To him the doorkeeper opens, and the sheep hear his voice; and he calls his own sheep by name and leads them out. And when he brings out his own sheep, he goes before them; and the sheep follow him, for THEY KNOW HIS VOICE"* (John 10:1-4).

God speaks to us in dreams and visions through angels. *"Then the Angel of God spoke to me in a dream, saying, 'Jacob.' And I said, 'Here I am' "* (Genesis 31:11). *"But while he thought about these things, behold, an angel of the Lord appeared to him in a dream, saying, 'Joseph, son of David, do not be*

*afraid to take to you Mary your wife, for that which is
conceived in her is of the Holy Spirit'''* (Matthew 1:20).

Although we published the following visions in our
book HOW TO HEAL THE SICK, we feel that they are so
pertinent for this end generation that we must repeat them
to you. We are careful not to follow prophecies by others,
because the Bible tells us we have access to the Father in the
name of Jesus, and that we are to follow after the Holy
Spirit. But we feel that these are true prophecies in the form
of visions, and that they are now being fulfilled and will be
totally fulfilled in the near future.

VISION BY FRANCES

In June of 1980, God gave me a vision of the
world with silver and gold bands covering the
entire globe — but not in the orderly sense you
would expect to see them. These bands were
spilling all over the world like melted silver and
gold rivulets and running into all sorts of odd
little places — mountains and valleys alike. There
was no obvious plan of any kind represented by
these silver and gold rivulets — they went hither
and thither all over the place. Sometimes they
were wide, and sometimes they were super
skinny. In some places it looked like a big blob of
melted silver and gold had fallen, but there was
no pattern of any kind! Then we saw people
begin to rise up and stand on these melted silver
and gold bands.

We began to ponder on this, because in the
beginning it seemed to us like nothing but a huge
hodge-podge, but slowly God began to reveal
what this vision meant, and how it applied

to our ministry.

The more we examined this divine vision, the more we began to understand that God was telling us to take the total message of salvation, which includes healing, to the entire world, by letting the masses learn how to operate in the supernatural and heal the sick.

Our hearts began to sing as God continued the revelation of what He wanted us to do. First, He directed us to teach on the subject of HOW TO HEAL THE SICK. We had seen students from the City of Light School of Ministry standing on the silver and gold bands, and thought momentarily that they were going to go to all parts of the world to teach the nationals how to heal the sick. Somehow this understanding did not give us total assurance that this was actually what the vision meant. We continued to think more about the vision.

Then the picture expanded even more, and we saw the video schools going into ALL the world — into the small places where evangelists never go, to teach all the people in the remotest places of the world how to lay hands on the sick and heal them. The students who learned from these video tapes would then go out and preach the gospel to the poor, heal the brokenhearted, preach deliverance to the captives and recovering of sight to the blind, and set at liberty those who are bruised.

For the first time, we plainly saw the identity of the students standing on the bands! We had seen students of all nationalities, but had thought they would be coming to the school here in Texas. Then we realized they were the ones we might not ever meet, the ones who might only see us through video tapes, but the ones who had received the message of how to heal the sick and had gone out to stretch forth their hands to the sick!

This is God's timing for another great move of His Spirit as the masses are being trained to go out and minister on a one-to-one basis. Bible colleges and schools of ministry have sprung up all over as a hungry world says, "Teach us how to operate in the supernatural the way the original disciples did!"

There is such a hungering among God's people to learn more about the things of God that we believe in a few years there will not be enough schools to fill the need, and the people will have to be put on a wait-list to get into the schools that are already in operation. What a thrilling thought, and what a thrilling time to be alive!

We were confident that God had opened our spirits to a dynamic, far-reaching mission of teaching the masses how simple it is to become a miracle-working disciple like those in the book of Acts.

As we held a Healing Seminar in Kansas shortly after this, Pastor Fred Kirkpatrick told us of a prophecy about the end times which literally exploded our faith as a confirmation of the part this teaching will play in what we believe to be the end of the end times before Jesus comes for those who love and obey Him.

Our book was ready for the typesetter with the exception of the introduction, when we contacted the publisher of a book entitled PERTINENT PROPHECIES I by John M. and Dorothea M. Gardner, and received permission to reprint the following prophecy, given by Tommy Hicks, noted evangelist, in 1961.

VISION OF THE BODY OF CHRIST AND THE END-TIME MINISTRIES

My message begins July 25, about 2:30 in the morning at Winnipeg, Canada. I had hardly fallen asleep when the vision and the revelation that God gave me came before me. The vision came three times, exactly in detail, the morning of July 25, 1961. I was so stirred and so moved by the revelation that this has changed my complete outlook upon the body of Christ, and upon the end-time ministries.

The greatest thing that the church of Jesus Christ has ever been given lies straight ahead. It is so hard to help men and women to realize and understand the thing that God is trying to give to his people in the end times.

I received a letter several weeks ago from one of our native evangelists down in Africa, down in Nairobi. This man and his wife were on their way to Tanganyika. They could neither read nor could they write, but we had been supporting them for over two years. As they entered into the territory of Tanganyika, they came across a small village. The entire village was evacuating because of a plague that had hit the village. He came across natives that were weeping, and he asked them what was wrong.

They told him of their mother and father who had suddenly died, and they had been dead for three days. They had to leave. They were afraid to go in; they were leaving them in the cottage. He turned and asked them where they were. They pointed to the hut and he asked them to go with him, but they refused. They were afraid to go.

The native and his wife went to this little cottage and entered in where the man and woman had been dead for three days. He simply stretched forth his hand in the name of the Lord Jesus Christ, and spoke the man's name and the woman's name and said, "In the name of the Lord Jesus Christ, I command life to come back to your bodies." Instantaneously these two heathen people who had never known Jesus Christ as their Savior sat up and immediately began to praise God. The Spirit and the power of God came into the life of those people.

To us that may seem strange and a phenomenon, but that is the beginning of these end-time ministries. God is going to take the do-nothings, the nobodies, the unheard-of, the no-accounts. He is going to take every man and every woman and He is going to give to them this outpouring of the Spirit of God.

In the book of Acts we read that "In the

last days," God said, "I will pour out my
Spirit upon all flesh." I wonder if we realized
what He meant when God said, "I will pour
out my Spirit upon all flesh." I do not think I
fully realize nor could I understand the fulness
of it, and then I read from the book of Joel:
*"Be glad then, ye children of Zion, and rejoice
in the Lord your God: for He hath given you
the former rain moderately, and He will cause
to come down for you the rain,
the former rain, and the latter rain —"* (Joel
2:23). It is not only going to be the rain, the
former rain and the latter rain, but He is going
to give to His people in these last days a double
portion of the power of God!

As the vision appeared to me after I was
asleep, I suddenly found myself in a great high
distance. Where I was, I do not know. But I
was looking down upon the earth. Suddenly
the whole earth came into my view. Every
nation, every kindred, every tongue came
before my sight from the east and the west, the
north and the south. I recognized every
country and many cities that I had been in, and
I was almost in fear and trembling as I beheld
the great sight before me: and at that moment
when the world came into view, it began
lightning and thundering.

As the lightning flashed over the face of
the earth, my eyes went downward and I was
facing the north. Suddenly I beheld what
looked like a great giant, and as I stared and

looked at it, I was almost bewildered by the sight. It was so gigantic and so great. His feet seemed to reach to the north pole and His head to the south. Its arms were stretched from sea to sea. I could not even begin to understand whether this be a mountain or this be a giant, but as I watched, I suddenly beheld a great giant. I could see His head was struggling for life. He wanted to live, but his body was covered with debris from head to foot, and at times this great giant would move his body and act as though it would even raise up at times. And when it did, thousands of little creatures seemed to run away. Hideous creatures would run away from this giant, and when he would become calm, they would come back.

All of a sudden this great giant lifted his hand toward the heaven, and then it lifted its other hand, and when it did, these creatures by the thousands seemed to flee away from this giant and go into the darkness of the night.

Slowly this great giant began to rise and as he did, his head and hands went into the clouds. As he rose to his feet he seemed to have cleansed himself from the debris and filth that was upon him, and he began to raise his hands into the heavens as though praising the Lord, and as he raised his hands, they went even unto the clouds.

Suddenly, every cloud became silver, the most beautiful silver I have ever known. As I watched this phenomenon it was so great

I could not even begin to understand what
it all meant. I was so stirred as I watched
it, and I cried unto the Lord and I said, "Oh,
Lord, what is the meaning of this," and I felt
as if I was actually in the Spirit and I could
feel the presence of the Lord even as I was
asleep.

And from those clouds suddenly there
came great drops of liquid light raining down
upon this mighty giant, and slowly, slowly,
this giant began to melt, began to sink itself in
the very earth itself, and as he melted, his
whole form seemed to have melted upon the
face of the earth, and this great rain began to
come down. Liquid drops of light began to
flood the very earth itself and as I watched this
giant that seemed to melt, suddenly it became
millions of people over the face of the earth.
As I beheld the sight before me, people stood
up all over the world! They were lifting their
hands and they were praising the Lord.

At that very moment there came a great
thunder that seemed to roar from the heavens.
I turned my eyes toward the heavens and
suddenly I saw a figure in white, in glistening
white — the most glorious thing that I have
ever seen in my entire life. I did not see the
face, but somehow I knew it was the Lord
Jesus Christ, and He stretched forth His hand,
and as He did, He would stretch it forth to
one, and to another, and to another. And as
He stretched forth His hand upon the nations

and the people of the world — men and women — as He pointed toward them, this liquid light seemed to flow from His hands into them, and a mighty anointing of God came upon them, and those people began to go forth in the name of the Lord.

I do not know how long I watched it. It seemed it went into days and weeks and months. And I beheld this Christ as He continued to stretch forth His hand, but there was a tragedy. There were many people as He stretched forth His hand that refused the anointing of God and the call of God. I saw men and women that I knew. People that I felt would certainly receive the call of God. But as He stretched forth His hand toward this one and toward that one, they simply bowed their head and began to back away. And each of those that seemed to bow down and back away, seemed to go into darkness. Blackness seemed to swallow them everywhere.

I was bewildered as I watched it, but these people that He had anointed, hundreds of thousands of people all over the world, in Africa, England, Russia, China, America, all over the world, the anointing of God was upon these people as they went forward in the name of the Lord. I saw these men and women as they went forth. They were ditch diggers, they were washerwomen, they were rich men, they were poor men. I saw people who were bound with paralysis and sickness and blindness and deafness. As the Lord stretched forth to give them this anointing, they became well, they became healed, and they went forth!

And this is the miracle of it — this is the glorious miracle of it — those people would stretch forth their hands exactly as the Lord did, and it seemed as if there was this same liquid fire in their hands. As they stretched forth their hands they said, "According to my word, be thou made whole."

As these people continued in this mighty end-time ministry, I did not fully realize what it was, and I looked to the Lord and said, "What is the meaning of this?" And He said, "This is that which I will do in the last days. I will restore all that the cankerworm, the palmerworm, the caterpillar — I will restore all that they have destroyed. This, my people, in the end times will go forth. As a mighty army shall they sweep over the face of the earth."

As I was at this great height, I could behold the whole world. I watched these people as they were going to and fro over the face of the earth. Suddenly there was a man in Africa and in a moment he was transported by the Spirit of God, and perhaps he was in Russia, or China or America or some other place, and vice versa. All over the world these people went, and they came through fire, and through pestilence, and through famine. Neither fire nor persecution, nothing seemed to stop them.

Angry mobs came to them with swords and with guns. And like Jesus, they passed through the multitudes and they could not find them, but they went forth in the name of the Lord, and everywhere they stretched forth their hands, the sick were healed, the blind eyes were opened. There was not a long prayer, and after I had reviewed the vision many times in my mind, and I thought about it many times, I realized that I never saw a church, and I never saw or heard a denomination, but these people were going in the name of the Lord of Hosts. Hallelujah!

As they marched forth in everything they did as the ministry of Christ in the end times, these people were ministering to the multitudes over the face of the earth. Tens of thousands, even millions seemed to come to the Lord Jesus Christ as these people stood forth and gave the message of the kingdom, of the coming kingdom, in this last hour. It was so glorious, but it seems as though there were those that rebelled, and they would become angry and they tried to attack those workers that were giving the message.

God is going to give to the world a demonstration in this last hour as the world has never known. These men and women are of all walks of life, degrees will mean nothing. I saw these workers as they were going over the face of the earth. When one would stumble and fall, another would come and pick him up. There were no "big I" and "little you," but every mountain was brought low and every valley was exalted, and they seemed to have one thing in common — there was a divine love, a divine love that seemed to flow forth from these people as they worked together, and as they lived together. It was the most glorious sight that I have ever known. Jesus Christ was the theme of their life. They continued and it seemed the days went by as I stood and beheld this sight. I could only cry, and sometimes I laughed. It was so wonderful as these people went throughout the face of the whole earth, bringing forth in this last end time.

As I watched from the very heaven itself, there were times when great deluges of this liquid light seemed to fall upon great congregations, and that congregation would lift their hands and seemingly praise God for hours and even days as the Spirit of God came upon them. God said, "I will pour my Spirit upon all flesh," and that is exactly this thing. And to every man and every woman that received this power, and the anointing of God, the miracles of God, there was no ending to it.

We have talked about miracles. We have talked about signs and wonders, but I could not help but weep as I read again this morning, at 4 o'clock this morning the letter from our native workers. This is only the evidence of the beginning for one man, a "do-nothing, an unheard-of," who would go and stretch forth his hand and say, "In the name of the Lord Jesus Christ, I command life to flow into your body." I dropped to my knees and began to pray again, and I said, "Lord, I know that this thing is coming to pass, and I believe it's coming soon!"

And then again, as these people were going about the face of the earth, a great persecution seemed to come from every angle.

Suddenly there was another great clap of thunder, that seemed to resound around the world, and I heard again the voice, the voice that seemed to speak, "Now this is my people. This is my beloved bride," and when the voice spoke, I looked upon the earth and I could see the lakes and the mountains. The graves were opened and people from all over the world, the saints of all ages, seemed to be rising. And as they rose from the grave, suddenly all these people came from every direction. From the east and the west, from the north and the south, and they seemed to be forming again this gigantic body. As the dead in Christ seemed to be rising first, I could hardly comprehend it. It was so marvelous. It was so far beyond anything I could ever dream or think of.

But as this body suddenly began to form, and take shape again, it took shape again in the form of this mighty giant, but this time it was different. It was arrayed in the most beautiful gorgeous white. Its garments were without spot or wrinkle as its body began to form, and the people of all ages seemed to be gathered into this body, and slowly, slowly, as it began to form up into the very heavens, suddenly from the heavens above, the Lord Jesus came, and became the head, and I heard another clap of thunder that said, "This is my beloved bride for whom I have waited. She will come forth even tried by fire. This is she that I have loved from the beginning of time."

As I watched, my eyes suddenly turned to the far north, and I saw seemingly destruction: men and women in anguish and crying out, and buildings in destruction.

Then I heard again, the fourth voice that said, "Now is My wrath being poured out upon the face of the earth." From the ends of the whole world, the wrath of God seemed to be poured out and it seemed that there were great vials of God's wrath being poured out upon the face of the earth. I can remember it as though it happened a moment ago. I shook and trembled as I beheld the awful sight of seeing the cities, and whole nations going down into destruction.

I could hear the weeping and wailing. I could hear people crying. They seemed to cry as they went into caves, but the caves in the mountains opened up.

They leaped into water, but the water

would not drown them. There was nothing that could destroy them. They were wanting to take their lives, but they could not.

Then again I turned my eyes to this glorious sight, this body arrayed in beautiful white, shining garments. Slowly, slowly, it began to lift from the earth, and as it did, I awoke. What a sight I had beheld! I had seen the end-time ministries — the last hour. Again on July 27, at 2:30 in the morning, the same revelation, the same vision came again exactly as it did before.

My life has been changed as I realized that we are living in that end time, for all over the world God is anointing men and women with this ministry. It will not be doctrine. It will not be a churchianity. It is going to be Jesus Christ. They will give forth the word of the Lord, and are going to say, "I heard it so many times in the vision and according to my word it shall be done."

Oh, my people, listen to me. According to my word, it shall be done. We are going to be clothed with power and anointing from God. We won't have to preach sermons, we won't have to have persons heckle us in public. We won't have to depend on man, nor will we be denomination echoes, but we will have the power of the living God. We will fear no man, but will go in the name of the Lord of Hosts!

Can you see what we see in these two visions given twenty years apart?

We believe now that God showed more in these two visions than we at first realized. The video schools continue to multiply and people all over the world are stepping out after learning how to operate in the supernatural. We believe God showed a telescopic vision of what He will be doing in even greater measure in this final end generation through ordinary people who will sell out to Him and serve Him without consideration of self or things of this world.

God used visions and dreams in many instances in the Bible to communicate with His servants. We have been blessed as God has given us both visions and dreams, but we believe the faithful Body of Christ will experience far greater visions and dreams in these very last days before the return of Jesus! Hallelujah!

CHAPTER 8

LOOKING BACK IN TIME
By Charles

Can we disciples of this end generation look back supernaturally into time?

Jesus did, so we should be able to do that, too, to accomplish what He wants us to do.

In the fourth chapter of John, Jesus was talking with the gentile woman at the well about living water when He said, *"Go, call your husband, and come here. The woman answered and said, 'I have no husband.' Jesus said to her, 'You have well said, 'I have no husband,' for you have had five husbands, and the one whom you now have is not your husband; in that you spoke truly. The woman said to Him, 'Sir, I perceive that You are a prophet'"* (John 4:16-19).

What did Jesus do for the kingdom of God by "looking back in time?"

"And many of the Samaritans of that city believed in Him because of the word of the woman who testified, 'He told me all that I ever did'" (John 4:39). We must remember at all times that when we shift gears from the

natural man into the Spirit realm, God gives this ability
to do His work. His work always is to save those who
are lost — to add to His kingdom those who love Him.

How was Jesus able to transcend the material
limitations of man and move backward in time? By the
Spirit of God, abilities or gifts are given to man which
fall into the limitlessness of God. *"Jesus Christ is the
same yesterday, today, and forever"* (Hebrews 13:8).

If Jesus did it while He was on earth as a man, we
can do it today, because He said we could. He was our
example, so in this end generation we disciples will be
doing this to perform the work of Jesus.

A few years ago a married couple came to me for
prayer. They said their marriage was beautiful and
perfect, except in their sex life she had a block where she
could not perform. Doctors and counselors search the
memories of people by probing with questions and can
often help those whose memories have been damaged or
warped by a traumatic experience of some kind.

I knew that I must not depend upon the limitations
of my flesh, but must ask God for this answer. I simply
moved from the arena of the flesh into the vast solar
system of God's knowledge, I shifted gears and my
spirit moved into the realm of God's Spirit world.

By opening my spirit and letting it search her past,
similar to letting my mind look back to remember
something, God let me sense that something happened
to her when she was between four and five years of age.
I asked her what had happened at that time. She could
not remember. I urged her to think carefully, because
God had focused His gift of the Spirit into that part of
her past so it had to be significant in relation to the

problem for which we were seeking the answer.

She still could not recall anything, when her husband said, "I know." He said her father had said to him just before they were married, "I must tell you something about my daughter. When she was four years old, I sexually molested her."

Something within her innocent mind, a fear or a wrong had been done which had set up a barrier toward men. It was not her fault, and yet it had been the work of Satan to block God's design for her life. But Satan's work was blotted out because God supernaturally uncovered the devil's hidden secret through an ordinary twentieth century disciple. Both the husband and wife believed when God allowed me to see backwards into time, just as the woman at the well believed because Jesus was able to transcend time.

When someone recognizes that God loves them enough to open the windows of heaven's knowledge through someone who has no way of knowing those secrets, miracles happen in the faith of that person.

A man called Frances when we were preparing to take a group of Christians to Israel and said his son was a mess and that he was sending him to Israel with us so we could straighten out his life. We couldn't straighten anyone's life in the natural, but we walk not after the flesh, but after the Spirit.

This young man, twenty-nine years of age, was slightly mentally retarded. Frances knew about this, but I didn't. When we were on the Mount of Olives, he threw away his cigarettes because God was already ministering to his spirit. We had just crossed the Sea of Galilee on a boat (we didn't walk across, but a deaf woman was healed on the boat as Frances commanded the deaf spirit to leave). We went into a restaurant in Tiberias for a "Peter's fish" dinner. Ten of us sat at a round table, and we had just sat down when I "looked intently at this young man."

My spirit mind sped swiftly from twenty-nine years of age backwards over the years when there seemed to be a brake, like a magnetic force, stop at age five. I asked the young man, "What happened between you and your father when you were five years old?"

He tried to recall, but could remember nothing. He said, "I remember when I was in the fifth grade in school that I left the classroom one day and the teacher said to the other students, 'That kid is stupid.'"

Can you see what must have entered that innocent boy's heart? He could not help it that his mind was not as normal as the other children. In his mind entered the hurt, the embarrassment, and perhaps resentment to imprint forever a scar that would further his problem. Satan moves about the earth, seeking those whom he can destroy, but God sent Jesus to redeem us from that curse.

I said, "That is significant, but it was when you were five years old that God wants to help you." He still could remember nothing, until the next morning he came to me excitedly saying, "I remember, I remember!" He said, "When I was about five, I remember that my mother and father were talking and didn't think I knew what they were saying. They said, 'We've got to get rid of that kid; we can't do a thing with him.'"

Can you imagine the blow to that little child's heart

when his parental security was being destroyed by Satan? Perhaps his parents didn't really say that with a wrong attitude, but he heard it that way in his heart.

This stroke of the devil drove his mental retardation further into the realm of darkness.

When he realized that the Almighty God had spoken to him (he didn't think of it as Charles speaking to him), God healed his mind and memory, and he was forever set free from the bondage of Satan! Glory to God!

When we disciples of this age need to do a miracle to further the kingdom of God, we are as unlimited as God Himself because by His Spirit we can shift gears and move into His vastness of knowledge!

One Sunday night I was sharing with our church on how to heal the sick and started to demonstrate by opening my spirit for a word of knowledge about a physical problem so God could be glorified with a miracle. Suddenly I turned to a man whom I had never seen before.

It was not a vision, but I began telling him about things he knew I had no way of knowing. I said, "About four years ago something happened in your life between you and a close member of your family. This caused you to turn from God and you have been in misery ever since and you are searching for a way out of this spiritual dilemma."

I don't remember other details, but for three or four minutes I looked into his past and told him all kinds of details he knew I couldn't know. He looked at me in awe and said, "How could you know all that? It has to be God."

What he said had happened was that his mother died and his father who was a minister of the Gospel had remarried. The father went into sin and completely left all relationship with God. This young man was also a preacher, and because of the tramatic spiritual death of his father, he, too, had his faith in God destroyed. He had gone into sin and left the ministry.

That night, because God let my spirit see into his past, he repented and turned his life back over to God. What a faith-building demonstration of the Spirit God gave the church when by His Spirit he allowed an ordinary human to move from the realm of the flesh into the great realm of the spirit world.

We disciples of this end generation have been given an awesome responsibility, but God never leaves us nor forsakes us. God will do anything within his perfect laws to reach the soul of one of his creation! Hallelujah!

By our human decisions we can choose to move into another world, into the spirit world where God says we live, to do the work of God. *"Not by might nor by power, but by My Spirit, says the Lord of hosts"* (Zechariah 4:6).

CHAPTER 9

LOOKING FORWARD IN TIME
By Charles

By the Spirit, man has throughout the Bible looked into the future, seeing ahead what God was doing for the redemption of mankind.

"God will accept all people in every nation who trust God as Abraham did. And this promise is from God himself, who makes the dead live again and speaks of future events with as much certainty as though they were already past" (Romans 4:17 TLB). The New King James version says, *"... calls those things which do not exist as though they did."*

"Behold, the former things have come to pass, and new things I declare; before they spring forth I tell you of them" (Isaiah 42:9).

God knows everything, past, present and future, and He is sharing with us in writing and by prophesy what He is going to do. It is only by the Spirit of God that man can look into future events before they happen, but God is doing that now, just as He did long ago in Bible days. God is glorified by the obedience of man and therefore He gives forth future information before it happens.

One of the beloved pastors with whom we have worked as evangelists for years was very pressed for $265,000 which was due within about sixty days after we were with him. We could tell this was a pressure upon him, although he is a man of great faith, and is building a very expensive church facility for which he needed this large sum of money.

During a service, Frances said, "Pastor, God says not to be concerned about the $265,000, for He will cause one man to come to you on the day the money is due and write you a check for $265,000.00. Thus says the Lord!"

It was thrilling to receive an exciting call from this Pastor on the day the money was due to be paid. He said, "Just at the last minute, a man came into my study and said, 'Pastor, how much did that lady say you would need today?'" The man wrote out a donation check for $265,000.00.

How can this happen in the twentieth century? Because God tells his disciples of this end generation things they need to know when they are fully trusting Him!

Jesus told us what would happen in this generation when He promised and foretold that signs and wonders would follow those who believe; and He further said to us, *"Follow Me!"* Jesus did many signs and wonders, and therefore we will do many signs and wonders when we follow Him and do His work!

Since Jesus is the same yesterday, today, and forever, He can take us back in time, forward in time, and

He can tell us what to do today. He said today is the day of salvation.

God's glory is on the earth today!

In the Old Testament, prophecies were almost all telling of the coming of Jesus to earth; some telling even further events in the future of God's calendar. The book of Revelation and some other places in the Bible are still unfulfilled prophetic events which WILL occur because God said they would. We can be very certain that every event predicted by God will come about exactly like God foretold and will be right on time!

Many men and women of God have been used in great ways to tell about the future, as well as seeing inside people's past by looking back in time.

What could God have ahead for us in these next few final years before Jesus comes for us?

We don't know, but we are expecting far greater things just ahead than we have seen in the past, and in God's perfect timing He will let us know what each of us are to do to perform our part of His plan.

CHAPTER 10

CHANGING WEATHER
By Charles

"And a great windstorm arose, and the waves beat into the boat, so that it was already filling. But He was in the stern, asleep on a pillow. And they awoke Him and said to Him, 'Teacher, do You not care that we are perishing?'

"Then He arose and rebuked the wind, and said to the sea, 'Peace, be still!' And the wind ceased and there was a great calm. But He said to them, 'Why are you so fearful? How is it that you have no faith?' And they feared exceedingly, and said to one another, 'Who can this be, that even the wind and the sea obey Him!'" (Mark 4:37-41).

Changing weather is not something that you do at your own prerogative. It is a supernatural action that can take place when you receive a rhema word from God! We question whether any human is wise enough to determine what weather is best or reasons for severe weather conditions, but we believe God will intervene for us and will tell us what to do about the weather.

Then we can command whatever God says and it will happen.

Can we change the weather when He wants it changed to display His power? Why not? We are His workmanship, and we are His servants who are to do His work on earth.

FROM GLORY: God has already done this in our lives, and we know He will do it in greater ways to get His greater work done soon. We are looking back at some of the spectacular miracles God has done in the past and are thrilled that we have His RECORDED GLORY in our books and articles.

Excerpt from our book IT'S SO SIMPLE (Formerly Hang Loose with Jesus) - Frances shares:

WOULD GOD DO IT FOR ME?

It's amazing how miniature our faith is at times — and it's amazing what God will do for us if we will just believe and trust!

I started driving from Anderson, Indiana, to Lafayette to speak at Purdue University at about 10 A.M. on a foggy, rainy day. As I drove along, it was almost impossible to see the road or the cars in front, and the only thing that made it possible to see the oncoming cars was their headlights. The fog kept getting worse and worse until I was just crawling along at about 15 miles an hour. The windshield wipers were going full speed but they still failed to keep the water off the windshield.

After I had gone over three sections of the highway which were covered with water, I began to panic and decided I had better find a gas station and call my husband who was auditing in Anderson to see if he felt I should come back. Then I said to myself, "That's silly, Charles isn't the one to ask, God is," so I said, "Lord, shall I turn around and go back?" Then I believe the devil got in the car with me and said, "Look, there won't be anyone coming out in Lafayette to hear you in such bad weather. Why don't you go back?"

However, I sure couldn't hear God speaking to me, so I continued. After another three or four miles, I really began to panic because it was almost impossible to drive. I desperately looked around for a little patch of blue in the sky when I stopped to fill up with gasoline, and couldn't see one tiny little spot that looked promising. I got back into the car and started on and began thinking to myself (or should I say to God?).

My conversation went something like this: "God, you couldn't stop the rain and turn the sky blue, could you?" I looked around again for a little sign of blue sky, but none! Then I continued "thinking to God," and I said "Now, Lord, I KNOW you could, because the Bible says you parted the Red Sea, and if you could part the Red Sea, and I know that you did, then I know that you could stop this rain and turn the sky blue."

Then the devil got in the car again (maybe he never got out) and said, "Well, sure he could turn the sky blue and stop the rain, but why should He do that for you? Who are *you?*" And I thought, "That's right, who am I to ask God for something like this?" Then another thought came into my mind ... "Who am I ? I'm God's girl—I'm a child of God and because I am God's girl, the Bible says I can ask for whatever I want, and it will be done!" (Matthew 21:22).

So very simply I said, "God, you know I can't see well enough to get through this rain, so would you please stop the rain and make the sky blue?" God's word says to trust Him, and that's all I did, but believe it or not, within 30 seconds the rain stopped, and within one minute the sky was blue and I drove all the way to Lafayette on dry highways and under blue skies. When I arrived at the university they asked me if I had noticed the tremendous change in the weather, and I related the story to them.

As I have retold this story in the area where it happened, I have always said, "Maybe you won't believe that God would be willing to do this for me, but I believe He loves me enough to do this for me, just like He loves *you* enough to do it for you, if you will only ask!" And in each service someone has come up to the microphone to tell the audience that they vividly remember the rain stopping and the sun coming out so suddenly on this particular Thursday. I think it's fabulous how

God always lets someone else see the miracles, too!

This story thrills me so much because it brings to mind the fact that God is still in the miracle-making business today just as He was when He stopped the sun, moon and stars for about 24 hours because of the prayer of one man. Joshua wasn't afraid to ask for the glory of God, so let's all start asking more!

In the same book, IT'S SO SIMPLE, Frances shares another weather story, but so different that it expresses God's versatility in miracles.

AIR CONDITIONED SHIELD

I never fail to get excited over the way God answers prayer. Sometimes it seems fervent prayer is so necessary before God hears and answers, and then sometimes the most simple little prayers will bring dramatic results!

After I had returned home from a long hard trip, I had a day and a half at home to get ready for another trip, and as I sat at my desk trying to get caught up on some of my correspondence, I kept feeling a tremendous tiredness—my legs ached, and my eyes felt like burned holes in a blanket, I had a headache but I continued working to the best of my ability, feeling confident of the fact that after another good night's sleep I would be in good shape for the trip.

I continued to feel more and more tired, and by the time I sat down to dinner, I could hardly eat, and in the middle of dinner, I said to my husband, "Honey, I'm so tired, I've got to go to bed!" And when I get up and leave my supper, you know there's something wrong!

I went right to bed and when he came to bed, he put his arms around me and instead of asking me how I felt, he said, "Honey, *you're sick!*" I was shocked because it had been many years since I had been sick, and I said, "I am?" And he said, "You're burning up with fever—no wonder your legs hurt, and no wonder your eyes feel like they're burned holes!" I said, "Charles, get me some aspirin, *quick!* I can't be sick, because I've got to catch the early plane in the morning for Oklahoma." Charles didn't move, or release his hold on me, but very softly he said, "Honey, wouldn't you rather pray?"

God's Holy Spirit really spoke to me, and I'm so glad that God uses my beloved husband's words to convict me when I'm wrong, and I said. "Sure, honey!"

Charles lovingly prayed this simple little prayer in which he asked for five things. He said, "Lord, she's your girl, so please touch her body and take away the fever and make her well, take away the pain in her legs, her headache, give her a good night's sleep so she'll wake up completely refreshed, and then, Lord, will you put a protective shield around her so she won't feel the heat as she goes to Oklahoma?" Then he simply said, "Thank you, Lord, for protecting your girl.''

I might have struggled for just one short second, but then it seemed as if God had just covered me with a protective coating, and I remember nothing else, but Charles told me this is what happened: Within just a few seconds my forehead had broken out with sweat, but before this happened, I had completely relaxed and was sound asleep. Then the sweat disappeared, and in less than a minute my forehead was as cool as could be because the fever was gone! I slept until 2:30 in the morning and when I woke up I told Charles I felt like I could have gotten up and tangled with tigers and come out the victor.

So many times we just fail to call on God *first*, and He's right there with his loving arms outstretched, just waiting to take care of us and protect us.

You might wonder what happened to the *fifth* request my husband made—for my protection from the heat. He asked this because I had been in Oklahoma two weeks earlier, and the intense heat had almost made me physically ill. The daytime temperature was running around 114 and the night wasn't much better. When I got to Oklahoma the next day, the temperature was 109 and it stayed there and above during my time there.

On Sunday afternoon I was standing out in the sun with another evangelist, and everyone was perspiring—the men's shirts were soaked down their backs — and someone said to me, "How come you're not perspiring at all?" I merely replied, "My husband prayed and asked God to shield me from the heat." The other evangelist turned to me and said, "Did you pray that too?" It was so amazing to see the two of us standing there (he even had his coat on) with no signs of discomfort or a sign of perspiration because we had both asked God to shield us. Even though our prayers were the same, they were sent up to God 1500 miles apart and yet God answered them both.

We must believe within our spirits the awesome authority and power Jesus has placed on our shoulders in doing His work to wrap up this phase of His ministry. We are blessed to be given this privilege of serving our great Master. We sense in our spirits so strongly that God has spoken to you and us as the Body of Christ that we have great accomplishments to attain and that it must be done very soon.

Just as God anointed Jesus without measure, so Jesus' anointing will be without measure on those who let Him freely live in them.

Another of the great miracles of weather changing was recorded in our book DON'T LIMIT GOD.

Charles:

On a trip to Canada, we had a tremendously exciting thing happen. It didn't look like it was going to be too exciting because as we flew in, an unexpected snow-storm came up. The winds were howling and whereas one week before, the temperature had been 93° in

Toronto, it was now 28° as we stopped to clear customs on the Canadian side. This was in the spring of the year when all the beautiful trees on the Niagara Peninsula were loaded with blossoms, and pear trees were blooming and beautiful, and all of the vineyards and the other fruit trees were covered with blossoms. It was a beautiful sight to behold, except for one thing. The snow was continuing to swirl and to come down, all the beautiful little blossoms were being covered with white snowflakes, and all of the green branches on the trees were turning white. The economy of the peninsula above Niagara depends largely upon the fruit crop each year. A freeze at this time could have had a devastating effect upon the economy of the entire Niagara Peninsula and many other areas of Canada as well.

The young minister who was driving us to the church where we were going to speak in St. Catharine's was telling us how the people depend upon the fruit crop for their livelihood for the entire year, and so we really began to pray for the fruit trees.

He pointed to the ice already forming on the blossoms of the fruit trees and said the weatherman had announced that the temperature would go down to the low 20's or upper teens and all the fruit crop would be destroyed.

In the back seat of the van God spoke ever so softly to me and said, "Take authority over the weather."

He didn't say when or how, but I HEARD GOD! When God speaks a rhema word to you it takes faith

only to know that it was God who said it and that He
actually did say it. There was no doubt in my heart that
He said it, so from that moment on it didn't take any
more faith; it just took obedience.

I whispered to Frances, "God said to take
authority over the weather." We didn't mention it to
the couple in the van with us, but we knew in our hearts
that God had a miracle waiting to happen. We were
excited to see when and how He would do it.

When we got to our motel room, we all felt we were
freezing because we had not anticipated weather of this
kind. We turned on the television to see what the
weatherman had to say. It was gloom, gloom, gloom,
gloom, GLOOM — nothing but GLOOM! All he could
talk about was the fact that it was going to freeze that
night and they were going to lose their fruit crop.

We dressed and went to the church for the service
that night. We worshipped God and praised Jesus in the
service, and then the associate pastor prayed for the
pastor's wife who had a bad back problem and had to
stay home because of the intense pain.

They turned the service over to us and we had
hardly started when God said, "Take authority over the
pastor's wife's back." We asked the congregation to
join us and we commanded the back to be healed and
the pain to go, in the name of Jesus. Then we turned to
the pastor and asked him to call his wife to see what
happened. We believe when we command a mountain to
be moved for God's purposes, it will move in the name
of Jesus!

The pastor went to his office and phoned his wife.
He came back about two minutes later, smiling with

excitement saying that all pain had left her back. We talked to him the next day and two weeks later and her back was totally healed.

As soon as he reported back that the miracle had happened, God said, "NOW, take authority over the weather!"

Again we asked the congregation to join their faith with ours and point their hands toward us. To me it was like I was relaying what God was saying. Jesus spoke with authority and with power, and with the same authority and the same power, I confidently spoke in the name of Jesus, "Weather, I COMMAND you to obey; snow, I COMMAND you to stop; freezing temperature, I COMMAND you to rise above freezing and command you not to damage one single blossom of the fruit, IN THE NAME OF JESUS!"

Then it was like an afterthought, but I know it was a postscript from God, I said, "Father, would you cause a warm gentle rain to fall and melt all the snow and ice so it will not damage the blossoms! Thank you Father, thank you Jesus!"

It was late that night when we left the church to go back to the van. When we walked outside there was a warm gentle rain falling, the snow which had left two or three inches on the ground before the service was all melted.

We anxiously turned the television set on the next morning for the report. The weatherman said, "We were lucky last night; a rain came and kept the fruit from freezing." We said, "That wasn't luck, that was God!" Then he said, "But we are expecting it to frost and freeze tonight because it has cleared, and that will likely freeze the fruit."

We commanded, "In the name of Jesus, Mr. Frost you will not freeze or damage this crop!"

We checked about two weeks later to get confirmation on the miracle, and were told that not a sign of damage came to the fruit in the whole valley.

The next summer we were in Florida and a couple came to us with the good report that they owned a large fruit orchard in the Niagara fruit belt and were at our service the night God told us to take authority over the weather. They said, "We had a bumper crop and how we praise God for His mighty miracle!"

Who am I to ask God to do something like this?

If God did it to show His glory and to fulfill His plan thousands of years ago, then for Jesus 2,000 years ago, why shouldn't He want to do the same thing today to fulfill His plan with us and through us? God is just as powerful today as He ever was or ever will be, and He will do whatever He needs to do to accomplish His work — through anyone who is willing to be His holy vessel.

How we praise you, Father, for your mighty miracles!

"Who can this be, that even the wind and the sea obey Him!"

CHAPTER 11

HEALINGS
By Charles

Healing miracles are happening so fast that it is hard to keep track of them. We thought it would be interesting to review some of our monthly newsletters where we have shared some of the miracles from our meetings. Would you like to hear a few of them?

MIRACLES MIRACLES MIRACLES MIRACLES

A doctor was brought from a convalescent home with multiple sclerosis who had not walked for seven years, and he almost ran down the aisle as God touched him!

Two women in wheelchairs got out almost simultaneously and hugged each other. One had never been to a Charismatic meeting before! The heavy steel brace was removed from her leg, and she walked up the stairs! Glory!

At St. Louis a man had broken his arm two years before and had never been able to straighten it out. God instantly touched him, grew the arm out approximately four inches and now he can bend it perfectly!

Thank you, Jesus!

A paragraph of healings: A lady with a steel hip socket and cane walked away walking like a model...A man who had a stroke and had one paralyzed side went home completely free of paralysis. By the next Sunday he was talking, walking, running, and living as normally as he had before the stroke...A woman wearing a brace was healed, took off the brace and has had no problems since then...A baby began to hear for the first time in his life...A woman with multi-vision in one eye was instantly healed!

A woman in a wheel chair breathing oxygen through a tube was instantly healed by God's power; two little girls being held by mothers standing side by side were healed of serious leg problems. One little girl was toed in so badly she fell over her feet. The other one had legs like jelly, and God instantly put strength in them, and both of them ran off as normal as any children we've ever seen.

A disintegrated spine was supernaturally put back together again...A heart was restored by the power of God including new arteries. The doctor confirms it's not the same heart! Rheumatoid arthritis crippled her and for the last seven years she has been confined to a wheelchair. She came expecting and one touch from Jesus, a command from Frances to rise up and walk, and her faith lifted her out of the chair and she was totally, instantly healed. She left the meeting, pushing her wheelchair, and running out the door!

We quit eating lunch long ago, and God has amazed us with the number of supernatural healings He has done during the lunch hour. Many times we see Him heal fifteen or twenty people. The other day in Michigan, a lady with partial paralysis from a stroke was healed; two ladies with M.S. were touched with the power of the Holy Spirit and walked up and down stairs, backs were healed, deaf ears opened, and on and on went the "lunch-hour" miracles!

The Spirit spoke to Frances the other night in a miracle service, telling her that a woman in the audience had been hemorrhaging for a long time and He was healing her. Quickly the lady came forward, and was overcome by the power of God. While she was under the power, God spoke to her, saying, "You will flood one more time and be healed." Just like the woman in the Bible who had an issue of blood for twelve years and touched the hem of Jesus' garment, so was this lady healed! GLORY!

I attended a meeting of yours two years ago and was healed of leukemia. I feel better than I have in ten years. I waited to let you know because I wanted to make sure it would last!

I have had internal bleeding for years, and you sent me a prayer cloth, and it instantly stopped. Praise God!

What a blessing to be in a miracle service! My back, arm and shoulder were all healed!

When you were here last year I was healed of a lump in my breast and another under the arm. I was also baptized in the Holy Spirit. Now I have the power to live the Christian life.

My son was healed of rheumatoid arthritis when you prayed for him last year. Praise God He still heals! He is now playing normally.

When you called out a word of knowledge about a

fractured skull that was healed, it was my mother's! She had fallen a year ago and her head had never healed or stopped hurting, and it was instantly healed!

My knees had been bothering me for 25 years, and when you touched them at the Full Gospel meeting, instantly all pain disappeared, and it hasn't returned since. Note: Over 50 knees were healed at the Atlanta meeting.

Thirty-two years ago I fell headlong down the stairs and rammed my head into the wall at the bottom, injuring my neck, back and elbow. On June 3rd when Frances had a word of knowledge about elbows, I claimed my elbow healing, but as I was standing in line, God said, "How about your back and neck? Didn't I heal them, too?" and praise God, He did!

I had arthritis in the back of my neck which caused muscle spasms and severe pain for years. When you were quoting scripture I felt a love enfolding my body. You stopped and said, "Someone was just healed of a severe neck problem." I haven't had a single pain or spasm since.

Two and a half years ago, my doctor gave me a letter stating as follows: "Present time patient is totally and permanently disabled." At your meeting in Evansville, I was totally and permanently healed and have no disability. Hallelujah!

I wrote to you last June asking you to pray for my husband who at that time had congestive heart failure, diabetes, and cancer and weighed 110 pounds. The doctors gave him no more than 90 days to live. Praise the Lord those prayers were answered. His diabetes was healed, there's no fluid in his lung and heart, and he now weighs 130 pounds. Thank the Lord!

A 20 months old baby had a large marble size hernia. It had been bound for six months with tape. The doctor told the mother he would need to do surgery on the baby at two years of age. Not only did the hernia heal, but the mother's right wrist ganglion was healed simultaneously. She had two previous ganlionectomies.

A lady with multiple sclerosis came forward, barely able to walk with a cane. She fell under the power of God, got up, held her cane up as she walked up steps, down steps and then walked all the way back down the aisle of the church unassisted.

Frances called out what she thought were three different words of knowledge: "Someone was injured 12 years ago. God has healed you. Come down here. Someone else has pain from an injury 17 years ago. You have been healed; come down here. Also, someone was hurt 22 years ago. God has just healed you. Where are you?"

One lady came forward and said she had been injured 12, 17, and 22 years ago; one time she fell off a cliff, another time was a head injury and the third time was an auto accident. God healed her of all three different injuries at once!

These extracts have been taken from just a few of our newsletters where we share monthly some of the exciting manifestations of God's glory!

Some healing miracles are more spectacular than others, but no matter how large or small, they all give glory to God and to Jesus!

Many times we call a word of knowledge for all who have knee problems to come forward for healing.

We have lined up over a hundred at one time, and we simply go down the line touching their knees in the name of Jesus and the power of God goes into them to perform the healings. Almost all of them are instantly healed. We remember two during the past year who had plastic knee caps in both knees, and when the power of God went in, the plastic was supernaturally removed and new kneecaps put in. Hallelujah!

A young man came to our service with such a bad heart the doctors had told him not only that he could never play football again, but that he only had a short time to live. When the power of God touched him, hc knew he was healed. He was examined by the doctor who said, "I see no reason why you shouldn't go play football right now!" Glory to God!

A lady came to Frances one day who had not been able to speak a sound for over fifteen years. God spoke to Frances and said the woman had witnessed a murder and could not reveal this to anyone. She had shut off her ability to speak, but through the supernatural works of God, she was set free and began to speak normally again!

A man came to us in Fairbanks, Alaska who had been in an accident a few years before which resulted in both feet and ankles being crushed badly. He had 102 fractures in his left foot and ankle and 104 fractures in the right. I held out his feet and commanded all the bones to come together in the name of Jesus. The power of God grew one leg out about an inch to make it even with the other, and his crooked feet straightened in front of his eyes.

I told him to test his feet. He got up, started to

walk, then began to leap and run and shout. He went all around the inside of the church running, leaping and praising God! Jesus is exactly the same today as He was 2,000 years ago — He is just living in ordinary people who believe, and doing the same miracles He did through Peter and James and the others in the first Church. How very much we love and praise our great and mighty God who always does things gloriously!

A young man was brought to one of our miracle services which we hold the third Thursday night of each month at the City of Light. The student at our school of ministry who had brought this young man apparently had done a great job building his faith to believe he would be healed that night, even though he had never seen a miracle.

He had been in a very bad head-on collision and the first damage he showed me was that his wrist was crushed and stiff and would not bend. I very simply rubbed my hand across his wrist, allowing the power of God to flow into him and then I told him to move his wrist in the name of Jesus. He looked rather questioning, but moved it slowly at first, then began to twist it, bend it and move his fingers freely. He said, "I can't believe it; it's perfect!"

Then I asked what other damages he had. His back had been so badly damaged that the doctor said he could never do any work that required lifting anything; his pelvic bones were fractured; his thighs were damaged, his knees were injured, and he had a screw holding his crushed ankle together.

In the mighty, powerful name of Jesus, I commanded every bone to be healed and his body

straightened. The power of God went through him and
he jumped up, bent every unbendable part of his body,
ran over and picked up a four or five year old boy, and
shouted that he was totally healed. No pain, no
stiffness, nothing but perfection done by the power of
God. How he praised God for this awesome spectacle!

The same night a lady was brought from San
Antonio, Texas, 200 miles away, on a stretcher. She had
a disease called scleroderma which causes the skin to
turn hard like a stone. This had turned the skin of her
legs and arms to "stone" and she was immobile; she
could neither bend her arms or legs or any part of them.

Frances simply reached out and took one of her
hands and said those marvelous words, "In the name of
Jesus!" and the stone turned to flesh!

She jumped off of the stretcher, began to run all
around the great City of Light dome, then outside,
down the stairs, up the stairs, back down and back up
about three times, and back into the church shouting
glory!

What a spectacular demonstration of God's glory
and His love for His people! What an awesome and
powerful and loving God we serve.

Many times God's power and glory is so strong in a
miracle service that we pray over the microphone and
just wave our hands over an audience and people are
healed. We recall one time when over 700 were healed at
one time within two or three minutes.

We were to share MY LOVE AFFAIR WITH
CHARLES in a large meeting and when we started to
the microphone, God spoke to me and said, "Tell the
people I am going to heal over 500 of them in three

minutes after you share this story. "We shared the beautiful miraculous love story of how we were divinely put together in marriage. Then we had the married couples restate their marriage vows and afterwards hold hands as we asked God to anoint their hands to minister healing to each other and their families.

We told them to lay hands on each other and as we prayed over the microphone and waved our hands over the audience, well over 500 were healed in the three minutes, just like God said He would do!

We have discovered that the "wind of the Holy Spirit" or the energy of God which does the healing can extend beyond our hands. One night Frances walked past a deaf man, probably no nearer than six feet from him, and his deaf ears instantly opened!

We have tested this unique flow of God's power away from the Spirit-filled person, and have discovered some very powerful results. People were healed when the shadow of Peter touched them. We believe that the reason was not only that their faith reached out to him, but that the power of God's Holy Spirit extended from within Peter into their sick bodies and healed them.

One night we were ministering in a church when over to our left in the front of the church there was a lady lying on a stretcher-like cot. She looked dead to us, but we discovered she did have life when we saw her toe moving to the beat of the music.

God spoke to Frances and she immediately spoke it to the congregation. She explained how the power of God flows like healing virtue and that God said four men of the audience were to pick up the cot and walk between a force field of power emanating from Frances

and me on one side and the two pastors on the other side
and that God would heal her.

We were told later that the woman had been
checked out of intensive care in a hospital 120 miles away
and she was told she would probably not live to get to the
miracle service, much less to get back to the hospital.

Four strong volunteers quickly came to the front of
the church, picked up the cot and slowly walked
through the wall of divine power flowing from the four
of us. They looked like pallbearers at a funeral, but we
knew they were walking toward a miracle of God.

They carried her through feet first, and when her
head went past Frances' body (she was last in the line),
Frances said those powerful words, "In the name of
Jesus Christ of Nazareth, rise up and walk!"

They laid the cot down and the woman jumped off
of it and ran all around the church shouting "Glory to
God, I'm healed." She never went back to her cot
because the wall of power went forth from modern day
disciples just like the same Holy Spirit power passed
from Jesus into the woman with the issue of blood. He
felt healing virtue flow from Him. That same healing
virtue comes from the same Holy Spirit who dwells
within us today!

There are great miracles done by God for His
people which are not healing miracles. Frances shared
one such mighty miracle in her book IT'S SO SIMPLE.
Frances:

GOD ON THE SPOT

Every so often my "prayer power" is really
put on the line by individuals. After my first
service at a camp meeting, a number of

ministers and laymen came up to me and said, "Frances, will you pray one of your 'dumb' prayers for us?" Without a moment's hesitation, I replied, "Certainly!"

Then they told me the following story: They had drilled a well during the past week and had hit beautiful spring water, but a rock had been sucked up into the pipe which was down 276 feet, and the water was shut off as a result. Two days of intensive working to get the rock out was to no avail. The well-digging company was coming the next day to take the pipe up, remove the rock and sink the pipe again at a tremendous expense. They asked me to pray and ask God to remove the rock.

Inwardly I think I groaned as I said, "Lord, they really put my faith on the spot, don't they?" And I had no more than said this when I realized they weren't putting me on the spot at all, they were putting God on the spot. At this moment the paraphrased scripture in Malachi came to my mind: "Try me, test me, prove me, and I will open the windows of Heaven and shower down blessings far greater than you can contain," and that's just exactly what I did.

A large circle had formed for the prayer, and I made a firm statement. "If there is anyone in this circle who doesn't believe that God can get that rock out of there, *get out of the circle*, because I don't want any unbelievers in it." Some stepped out, and when the circle was re-formed, I merely prayed this simple little prayer: "God, this is your money. You can spend it to have the pipe taken up and put down again, or you can use it to win souls to Jesus Christ by merely getting the rock out. I don't know how you're going to do it, Lord, but thank you anyway."

Right now I'm wondering if I even believed it myself. There are times when I pray automatically because this is what I *know* God wants me to do, and I don't believe I even think at the moment as to whether or not He will do it, I only know that His Holy Spirit has told me to pray.

Just then a pastor came up and asked me to go and pray for an individual with multiple sclerosis, and while I was walking to the car, I heard a mighty shout go up — they had turned the pump on, and the water was shooting out like a fire hose! *No more rock!*

The fabulous thing about God is we never really understand how He works — we just know that He does!

We have seen tens of thousands, if not hundreds of thousands of healings during the short few years we have had the baptism with the Holy Spirit, some small, some great, but all of God! This is just a quick panorama of God's glory as we soared over a short period of the past. Think of the glory of God just ahead as we look forward with eyes of faith to the greater things Jesus will be doing through the totally yielded Body for this end-time ministry of the Holy Spirit.

We estimate that up until a year before the writing of this book, approximately 20% of the people we ministered to were healed miraculously. Then it was as if God turned a page in a book one night and about 95% were instantly healed! We talked about this fantastic night of miracles and said, "God, would you let this happen again sometime?"

God gives exceedingly, abundantly more than we could ever ask or dream, and He has never stopped this giant flow of miracle healings. We continue night after night to see 80 to 95% healed. We will never be satisfied until 100% are healed, because this often happened to Jesus, and He said we would do the same things He did, and even greater things!

Glory...glory...glory...and on and on goes the glory of God and Christ Jesus as they swiftly move toward the end...from glory to glory!

CHAPTER 12

HOLY SPIRIT COMMUNICATION
By Charles

God has had an unbroken line of communication with His people throughout all the ages, and what is happening today is no different than what occurred in Bible days.

We have had the thrill of God speaking or telling us something directly by the Spirit in many different ways.

Why does God speak often to some and seemingly never to others? God speaks to everyone, but in order to hear Him we must want to obey Him with all our hearts, souls, minds, and bodies. A total and complete commitment of our lives to Him is necessary so He can do what He wants to through us. Self must be put completely aside so that we can follow after the Holy Spirit and not after our own desires. Then we will hear the voice of God when He wants to communicate with us.

"*'Surely the Lord our God has shown us His glory and His greatness, and we have heard His voice from the midst of the fire. We have seen this day that God speaks with man; yet He still lives'''* (Deuteronomy 5:24).

As surely as God spoke to Moses, so He will speak just as clearly to His Moseses of this generation, for God's work still goes on and will continue until mankind is redeemed according to His plans. Sometimes He speaks audibly, sometimes silently. *"God, who at various times and in different ways spoke in time past to the fathers by the prophets, has in these last days spoken to us by His Son, whom He has appointed heir of all things, through whom also He made the worlds"* (Hebrews 1:1, 2).

To have God speak to us audibly or silently through Jesus is an awe-inspiring event! This I know personally because in 1969 I was supernaturally blessed when I heard Jesus speak to me in two different ways in one night!

I was sitting in a chair with my back about three feet from a window when I heard Jesus speak through my hearing mechanism just as plainly as I have ever heard the voice of any man. It was awesome to realize that the Almighty God, through Jesus, who spoke to Moses and many others in the Bible, spoke just the same way to an ordinary businessman among three million people in Houston, Texas. This story is told in detail in our books PRAISE THE LORD ANYWAY and BORN AGAIN, WHAT DO YOU MEAN?.

In the same night that God audibly spoke to me, I was praising Him from the depth of my heart for doing such an awesome thing for me, when I asked Him for a small thing. He answered me this time, not through my ears but directly into my mind. It did not come as a

thought, but as words spoken by the Spirit of God —
soundless words, but as clearly heard as if it had come
through my human hearing mechanism. God said,
"Charles, let Me do this My way." This was repeated
three times within less than an hour as I asked three
times for some insignificant thing.

This was one of the greatest miracles of my life and
the words he spoke, "Charles, let Me do this My way",
have guided my life from that time to this. Whatever
God wants to do with My life, I guarantee I want to do
it His way.

We believe God will be doing far more of this type
of communication between now and the return of Jesus!
We need to gird up our loins to be ready to hear God
any time He speaks to us, and be willing to respond
without questioning Him.

*"Oh, that they had such a heart in them that they
would fear Me and always keep My commandments, that it
might be well with them and with their children
forever!"* (Deuteronomy 5:29).

God's presence and His glory will be upon us when
we always keep all His commandments with all our
hearts!

Another exciting way God supernaturally
communicated with us was during a mountain-top
retreat. We traveled a long distance by car and finally
arrived in mid-afternoon. We were tired and wanted to
rest, so we asked if it would be possible for someone to
knock on our door at five o'clock to wake us up. The
motel was a long, single row of rooms and we were just
about in the center. We had a tiny room and our bed
was just one step away from the door.

We were in a deep, sound sleep and were awakened when we heard a knock on the door. I instantly jumped out of bed, took the one step to the door and opened it. No one was there! I looked in each direction, but there was not a single person in sight. I checked my watch and it was exactly five o'clock.

We both started dressing, wondering how the girl who had knocked on our door disappeared so rapidly, when at 5:05 o'clock we heard another knock on the door. We opened it and the girl said, "I'm sorry I'm five minutes late."

We said, "Didn't you knock just five minutes ago?" and she said, "No!" Well, then who had knocked on the door? Could it be that God had sent an angel to wake us up exactly on time? We will always be on time when we listen for His instructions to do His work, because He will always be exactly on time.

Upon another occasion, we flew into a city, rented a car and drove about sixty miles to the town where we were having a crusade. As we were driving Frances said, "Should we just keep the car and drive on to West Virginia tomorrow instead of going back sixty miles and then flying over?"

I had seen a small map of the United States and it looked too far to drive, so I said, "Let's just go back because it would be too hard to drive that far before the service tomorrow."

After we got into the motel, Frances again said, "Don't you think we should drive tomorrow? When you go to the motel office, check the mileage chart." I forgot to look.

Later that night Frances again said, "Charles

don't you think we should just drive tomorrow?'' I said, "Let's think about it, but it still looks too far."

The next morning as we were eating breakfast, Frances AGAIN repeated the statement that she felt we should check the mileage chart. Again I forgot, so we got into the car, drove the sixty miles back to the airport, turned in the rental car, checked in for our seat assignments and walked to the waiting room. After sitting there for a short while we heard a plane circling the airport but not landing. Before long, it sounded as though it was going off to another destination. Then we heard the announcement, "Sorry, but the fog prevents the plane from landing so the flight to West Virginia is cancelled!"

We quickly ran back to the rental car desk, got exactly the same car we had just turned in, drove back the same sixty miles we had just come over and had to rush driving all the way to West Virginia, and were still thirty minutes late getting to the meeting!

What had happened? Frances was responding to a little nudge from the Holy Spirit and I wasn't tuned in as finely as she was. Next time we are both going to be more sensitive to do what God says!

In the end times, God will speak in many ways, but we must train our spiritual ears to hear the slightest sound of His voice. We will need to be super sensitive and so finely tuned in that we will not be distracted by the devil's tactics to cause delays and other attempts to divert us from God's work.

As we have relived some of the supernatural experiences that have changed our entire lives, we wonder what would have happened if we had not been

willing to believe that we actually heard the voice of God.
Frances:

God spoke to both of us before we were married
and told us the exact minute, time and place where we
were to be married. When God spoke to me, I could
have questioned Him, because I had said for years after
I was saved that I was going to have such a mad, wild
love affair with God that there would never be room in
my life for a husband! Could I have misunderstood God
about getting married?

I could have mentioned to God that I was older
than Charles! Charles could have had the same question
in his mind!

I could have been doubtful about the two of us
living 1,200 miles apart! Who would give and take in the
moving arrangement? Could he continue his work as a
CPA and let me travel all over the country fulfilling the
call of God on my life? Did I stop and leave the ministry
God called me to?

What would a man do who had never had children,
when he was faced with a sixteen-year-old daughter and
a married son? Could he cope with a teenager in the
house when he was used to peace and quiet at all times?
What would he do when she brought home a houseful
of noisy teenagers?

Thousands of questions might have plagued us at
that time had we not both been sure we heard the voice
of God. There was no doubt in the mind of either of us
that God had spoken, and we had no choice except to
obey! And obey we did!

I just looked at Charles across the room and said,
"Honey, can you imagine our lives if we hadn't heard

and obeyed that small still voice that told us to get married?'' Charles' eyes bubbled with tears as he threw me a kiss across the room and said, ''No, I can't imagine our lives without each other!''

Many years ago in a Southern Baptist Church each of us heard God speak at the same time and He told us that we were to have a miracle service in that Baptist church Tuesday night.

We could have said, ''But, God, we never had a miracle service. What would we do?'' But we didn't.

We could have said, ''But what if nobody gets healed?'' But we didn't.

We could have said, ''But there's not time enough to publicize it!'' But we didn't!

There were many things we could have said, but we said none of them. We only said what God had told us to say and that is that we were going to have a miracle service Tuesday night! And what a miracle service it was! What would we be doing today if we had not been listening intently enough to have heard God about starting a miracle ministry?

Walking through an airport, holding hands, and not talking to each other, but thinking to God and listening, we both heard God tell us that Charles was to leave his CPA practice in two weeks.

We could have said, ''But how will he support us if he leaves his business?'' But we didn't.

We could have said, ''But what will happen to the company?'' But we didn't.

We could have said, ''But it takes longer than that to leave a company where you are the president.'' But we didn't!

We just did what God said, and believed that He would supply our every need, and He has! What would have happened to our ministry where we are together twenty-four hours a day, if we had failed to respond to that small voice of God? He didn't shout, He didn't even speak audibly, but it was so quiet and soft we could have missed Him if we had not had our antennae up to pick up the slightest command from Him.

We all need to have our track shoes on today so that we can start running at the slightest signal from God, and not have to waste time. We need to keep the whole armor of God so polished at all times that we are always ready to hear and obey, because what He is going to be saying to the Body of Christ in these days is going to be heard only by those who listen carefully day and night. But what a blessing to be tuned in and begin to hear that voice that is so indescribable and so magnificently incredible in what it says to us!

Saul had just seen Jesus on the road to Damascus and was blinded. Jesus had said to him, *"'Saul, Saul, why are you persecuting Me?' And he said, 'Who are You, Lord?' And the Lord said, 'I am Jesus, whom you are persecuting...arise and go into the city, and you will be told what you must do'"* (Acts 9:4-6). Then Jesus said to Ananias in a vision, *"Arise and go to the street called Straight, and inquire at the house of Judas for one called Saul of Tarsus, for behold, he is praying. And in a vision he has seen a man named Ananias coming in and putting his hand on him, so that he might receive his sight"* (Acts 9:11, 12).

The Lord had to speak to Ananias a second time, because he said, *"Lord, I have heard from many about*

*this man, how much harm he has done to Your saints in
Jerusalem. And here he has authority from the chief priests
to bind all who call on Your name"* (Acts 9:13, 14).

When Jesus told him the second time, *"Go, for he
is a chosen vessel of Mine to bear My name before
Gentiles, kings, and the children of Israel. For I will
show him how many things he must suffer for My
name's sake"* (Acts 9:15, 16). Ananias obeyed!

As a result of his obedience, even in great fear, the
great Paul was not only healed, but he received the gift
of the Holy Spirit and his calling into the ministry of
reconciliation. The Pauline epistles might not ever have
been written if Ananias had not obeyed, even if it meant
suffering for the Lord Jesus Christ.

If we are to be chosen instruments of Jesus in these
last days before His return, we must not only be
sensitive, but willing to face any danger and even suffer
for His Name's sake! Are you willing? We not only are
willing, but anxious to do all that He calls us to do!

Even though Ananias had heard about Paul
harming the Christians, he knew the voice of the Lord
and he went as instructed.

What would have happened if Ananias had not
been sensitive to the voice of Jesus? Jesus had told
Ananias, *"Go, for he is a chosen instrument of Mine, to
bear My name before the Gentiles and kings and the
sons of Israel; for I will show him how much he must
suffer for My name's sake"* (Acts 9:15, 16 NASB).

If we are to be chosen instruments of Jesus in these
last days before his return, we must not only be
sensitive, but willing to face any danger and even suffer
for His name's sake!

CHAPTER 13

BAPTISM WITH THE HOLY SPIRIT
By Charles

"'And it shall be in the last days,' God says, 'That I will pour forth of My Spirit upon all mankind;'" (Acts 2:17 NASB).

God is doing that like a waterspout from heaven in these very days in which we live!

As we travel around the world, preaching the Gospel with signs following, we are seeing multitudes receive the wonderful and powerful infilling of God's Holy Spirit. It is almost a daily experience for us to see 120 receive the baptism with the Holy Spirit. Even if we stay two or three days in the same church or auditorium, people almost run when we make a call for the baptism with the Holy Spirit. The world is hungry for the Presence and Glory of God to be evidenced in their lives, so when they see a flow of miracles and a demonstration of His Spirit and power, they are convinced that this is that which Joel prophesied long ago.

At the Constitution Hall in Washington, D.C. we

saw about 1,200 receive the baptism with the Holy Spirit
in one service with the evidence of speaking in tongues.
This is ten times the number who received on the Day of
Pentecost.

In Pennsylvania the ushers counted over 1,000 who
received in one night. It is so easy for hungry and thirsty
people to receive, and God's people are wanting this
NOW!

We had just met Pastor Buck (ANGELS ON
ASSIGNMENT) for the first time immediately prior to
our first service in his church. The singers and musicians
were singing about the Day of Pentecost and had a
musical instrument which sounded like wind, and God
spoke to me — "Minister the baptism right now!"

Frances was sitting between Pastor Buck and me,
so I whispered to her and she relayed the message to
Pastor Buck, asking if that was all right with him. He
said, "Be my guest!"

We stepped to the microphone, spoke for maybe
five minutes telling them what God had just said, and
about 400 people rushed to the front of the church
auditorium to be a living, modern part of the Day of
Pentecost in that beautiful church! There was no
begging, no urging, no coercing, no pleading — just an
opportunity for another host to be endued with the
power of God during these days when prophecy is being
fulfilled daily!

Recently we ministered for one Sunday morning
and three successive Sunday nights in Bob Tilton's great
Word of Faith World Outreach Center in Dallas, Texas.
Over 2,200 received the baptism with the Holy Spirit!
One night at the very beginning of the service we made

the call to receive God's gift and over 600 came and received!

Our book, THE TWO SIDES OF A COIN, has been used to minister to tens of thousands around the world. People constantly come to us telling how they were wanting to know more about this "mysterious" event that was happening in the lives of many, and someone gave them a copy of THE TWO SIDES OF A COIN. This simple story of how God broke down religious teachings in our lives opens the door into the supernatural world when they see how ordinary, simple, and easy this is.

God told us soon after we received the baptism with the Holy Spirit to take the mystery out of the supernatural for His people. One man stated what he saw in our ministry, "You take the mystique out of the supernatural, but leave it holy."

God's Word and His ways are simple so that anyone coming to Him, even as a little child, can understand. So many people want to leave everything up to God, but God wants to leave most of His earthly power and actions up to us. People try to work up emotions, tarry, plead, beg, struggle, and try to be something which they are not to receive this gift from God. God created us in His own image, so we urge people receiving to be like God created them and receive what He has for them.

Early in our Spirit-filled ministry we discovered that people needed to realize that when they asked Jesus to baptize them with the Holy Spirit, He would do His part immediately, but they themselves would have to do the earthly, human part. It was the fishermen, tax collectors, and other ordinary people who spoke in tongues on the Day of Pentecost. Mary, the mother of Jesus, was also in that group. When we simply believe and begin to love God with the faith of a little child and make little sounds, the miracle will happen. The sounds must continue to be made (not just two or three), and made rapidly so our minds won't keep trying to control our spirits, and God will give the language of the Spirit. Our spirits don't need to think like our minds do, and when we act upon the human part, the springs of living water will flow forth from our innermost being. God and man work together beautifully when we realize that God doesn't need to change us into something we are not — He just wants us to be filled with His Spirit so He and Jesus can live in us! You may not minister the baptism the way we do; that's all right because it is Jesus who gives the Spirit to us!

Many times people are just loving God in the quietness of their home, and begin to speak with other tongues. They don't need instructions, but to most people instructions take away the mystery and give them understanding of how to do their part. It is so easy to get hungry people to pray a sinner's prayer and get saved, and it is just as easy to instruct someone on how to receive the gift of the Holy Spirit.

The other night a woman called us and needed help. Frances discerned that what she really needed was the power of the Holy Spirit, and ministered in moments over the phone.

Several deaf-mutes have received the baptism in our services. One night in California while we were ministering to a group, someone began speaking so loudly in tongues that I thought they were emotional and out of order. I don't let people disturb others that way, and was about to ask her to be quiet, when I saw that she was a deaf-mute girl to whom the pastor had introduced us before the service.

The Spirit of God had ministered to her and she began to loudly speak with her Spirit language. The pastor began to weep with great joy and told us he had been in Pentecost for over sixty years, and had only seen this happen one time previously!

One night we were ministering the baptism with the Holy Spirit to a group, among which was a man 92 years old. He was so excited that before the rest received, I pointed to him and said, "The glory of God is upon you." He fell under the power of God and began fluently speaking in tongues. He could hardly stand on his feet the rest of the evening and the next day. He was healed that night as God supernaturally touched him.

God is pouring out His Spirit mightily on people of all ages, all denominations, and in all walks of life.

Our little granddaughter Charity was carried onto the stage in Fort Worth, Texas, when she was about a year old. Grandma asked her where Jesus lived and she unhesitatingly patted her heart, even though she had not yet learned to talk.

Because she understood about Jesus and had been born again, our daughter Joan and son-in-law Bob laid hands on her when she was two years old to receive the baptism with the Holy Spirit. One day when she was two-and-a-half she was sitting on my lap when I spoke in tongues. She tilted her little head and said, "Holy Spirit" and out of her innermost being flowed rivers of living water as she, too, spoke fluently in tongues.

Her little sister Spice followed in the footsteps of Charity when she, too, was two-and-a-half. Grandma was playing with her and Spice said, "Grandma!" Frances said, "What, Spice?" Out of little Spice came a flow of tongues as fluently and beautifully as we have ever heard. Frances said, "Spice, are you speaking in tongues?" Spice said, "Yea!"

Frances asked Bob if he had laid hands on Spice for the gift of the Holy Spirit and Bob said, "No, Charity did!"

Jesus said in Mark 16:17, *"And these signs will follow those who believe: In My name they will cast out demons; THEY WILL SPEAK WITH NEW TONGUES."*

While Peter was still speaking these words, the Holy Spirit fell upon all those who heard the word. And those of the circumcision who believed were astonished, as many as came with Peter, because the gift of the Holy Spirit had been poured out on the Gentiles also. For they HEARD THEM SPEAK WITH TONGUES AND MAGNIFY GOD" (Acts 10:44).

Even these tiny children who had been raised in an atmosphere of praise and worship of God shifted gears and stepped into the supernatural world and received this great miracle from God. It is not uncommon now that they are older (Charity is six and Spice three at the time of this writing) for them to lay hands on the sick and see them recover just like Jesus said, without reference to age, denomination or anything except, "Those who believe will...speak with other tongues...lay hands on the sick and they will recover."

We are the disciples of this end age and we will see greater things happen today than the disciples of the early Church saw! This is the time to enter into the dimension of the Spirit world and live to the fullness of the expectation of Jesus. He wants us to step into our position and speak with great boldness and we, too, will see buildings shake because of His power!

CHAPTER 14

THE WIND IS BLOWING AGAIN
By Frances

The supernatural power of the wind of the Holy Spirit is not limited by time, space, or numbers and is an awesome thing to watch. It has two different effects upon people. *"By fearful and glorious things (that terrify the wicked, but make the godly sing praises) do You answer us in righteousness..."* (Psalm 65:5 AMP).

There are many people, indeed Christians, who are afraid of the power of God, and then there are those who sing praises unto God when they see the supernatural. The supernatural either attracts or repels!

Charles and I are in the "attracts" category, because we have both loved the supernatural from the moment of our conversions. Maybe it was because in my own life God started me off with the supernatural that I have always been fascinated with what God can do.

I remember vividly the eye operation that started my search for God. I had gone to the hospital and I certainly was not a Christian, even though I had attended church for a major portion of my life. I did not even know how to pray.

I had read the first verse of the 23rd Psalm, and no more, because this was a short operation, and I decided that was a sufficient amount to read when such a short time was involved. Then I made a great decision to give God a "break" and pray.

"I laid the Bible aside because I felt that was enough reading, and started to pray — even though I hadn't prayed since my last operation. Doesn't everyone pray in a time of crisis?

"I really prayed.

"I said, 'Oh, God, don't let the operation hurt tomorrow. I can stand anything, but don't let it hurt when they operate on my eye.' I did what we all do -- I really ignored God during good times, and then ran screaming for help when the tide went against me!" (From my book GOD IS FABULOUS).

In a split second of time, the thought came into my mind that I had not read the first verse of the 23rd Psalm, but had quoted it, and something told me to pick up my Bible again and look to see what it actually said.

God knows how to deal with each and every one of us in the way that will reach us the best, so God dealt with me in the area of printing, since I owned a printing shop. Any printer knows that once the ink is laid down on a piece of paper, there is no way that you can successfully get it off again, and as I opened my Bible, the page where the 23rd Psalm had previously been, was absolutely white! There was no printing of any kind on it. Then I saw the finger of God write five words in the brilliant red blood of Jesus Christ across the blank pages in my Bible. He wrote, "Frances Gardner, (that was my name then) I LOVE YOU."

"I think in one world-shattering moment I got a glimpse of what my life had been -- a constant, 'Oh, God, YOU do this for me!' And never a thought as to what I could do for Him.

"I didn't know what I was doing really, but in that moment I said, 'God, I take back that prayer, and I don't care how much it hurts tomorrow, but I promise You this. When I get out of this hospital, I will spend the rest of my life seeing what I can do for Jesus Christ, and not what He can do for me.'

"Little do we realize what we say in times like this, and how much truth is spoken during trials and tribulations." (From my book GOD IS FABULOUS).

I have never been the same from the day that God wiped the printing off of the pages of my Bible and put his words written in blood indelibly upon my very heart. They were burned there forever.

Because I had responded to the supernatural, God dealt again in an extremely supernatural realm where martinis in my life were concerned. Martinis had never been a real problem with me, because the grace of God saw to it that I had no tolerance for alcohol, but I wonder what might have happened to me if God had not intervened.

I suddenly lost my taste for martinis, and for a baby Christian, there can be a problem in saying "No, thanks, I don't drink!"

I had gone over to the house of some friends of mine and the husband thought I had flipped my wig and become a "religious fanatic," and he insisted that I take a martini after calling me "Holy Josephine!"

I didn't want it, and didn't know what to do or say. I felt like I was backed into a corner and didn't know how to fight my way out, so I silently screamed to God and said, "God, shall I drink it to be sociable?" (and I didn't want it) "...or should I pick it up and hold it" (and that's compromise, and God doesn't honor compromise)...or should I just say, "No, thank you, I don't drink?" I didn't know what to do, so I just made the fastest prayer you ever heard, and God answered me in such a supernatural way, there was no doubt in my mind as to His answer.

When I opened my eyes, God had turned the martini into a snake, the sign of evil in the Bible! God had clearly let me know that alcohol had no place in my life.

I looked up and said, "No thank you, I don't drink!" and as soon as I said that, the snake turned back into a martini! That is the last time anyone has ever offered me a drink. God had dealt with me in a supernatural realm, and I didn't question it, or argue with Him, nor was I terrified. I was just grateful that He had given me such a clear, definite answer!

After Charles and I were married, and we were traveling across the nation sharing the love of Jesus Christ, we heard some peculiar things about a woman named Kathryn Kuhlman. We heard that people had dramatic healings in her services and when they came forward to testify, she "pushed them over!" This did not turn us off! Instead, it put a hungering in our hearts to see what this was that people were beginning to talk about.

We were in the Pittsburgh area, and heard more and more about this unusual woman, and a desire was created in our hearts to see what she really did to people! We read the newspaper and discovered that the next morning she was to be at the First Presbyterian Church, and a friend of ours volunteered to take us. We got there in plenty of time, but the crowd was so great, it was obvious that many were going to be shut out. We prayed fervently, asking God to let us get in, if he had a purpose in our being there, but if not, to let in the sick and afflicted. Just as the doors were beginning to close, we saw a little girl next to us who looked only a step away from death, and Charles and I both instinctively prayed, "God, if it's her or us, let her in, because she needs it more than we do!"

We stepped back to let her family ahead of us and then we heard an usher say, "Charles and Frances Hunter, will you step this way, please?" We could hardly believe our ears, but immediately stepped out and followed the usher to a seat in the second row. God wanted to be sure we could see everything clearly!

We watched things we had never seen before. We saw dramatic divine healings of all kinds — a deaf mute healed, the little girl we had prayed God would let in before us was healed, and we saw things first hand that we had heard about. When they came forward to testify of their healing, we noticed Kathryn Kuhlman just laid her hands on them and they all fell backwards. We had previously heard of this, and I felt it must be for weaklings or something. Either that, or she pushed them over! When I saw Kathryn Kuhlman for the first time, I realized she wasn't big enough to push anybody over, and yet here I was sitting in the second row and watching as many as 6 or 8 people all falling "under the power" at the same time. I couldn't understand it, but I still wondered if there wasn't some kind of a trick connected with it.

All of a sudden Kathryn left the podium and announced that the power of God was so strong He didn't need her there, so she said she was going to do something that she normally didn't do. She was going to walk down the center aisle, and she asked that no one touch her and she also asked that no one come out of their seat until she called them. She came down to the second row and turned to the seat across the aisle from where we were. She saw a friend of hers and motioned for him to come out. He's bigger than she is, so I decided she couldn't very well push him over. She laid her hands on him and just said, "Jesus, bless him" and this big man fell over backwards. I looked at him real good, and he looked like he was enjoying whatever was going on. The ushers helped him to his feet, and again she laid her hands on him, and again, down he went! I couldn't believe my eyes, and then I looked directly at Kathryn, and saw she was pointing her long slender finger, and on the end of that finger was ME! I decided I was bigger than she was, so I stepped out. She just laid those soft hands on my temples ever so gently and asked God to bless me, and bless me He did, because would you like to guess where I was? Right on the floor! And in my best dress besides, knowing I had to speak at a luncheon that day! I could have cared less. I felt as if I was in heaven. The Spirit of God had breathed on me and I felt like a feather as I went down! I have never been the same!

On the way home from Pittsburgh, I opened my Bible to the 18th chapter of John and began reading, and you'd never guess what I discovered! An interesting verse that I knew God had just put in the Bible that very afternoon because I had never see it before. Verses 4-6 read: "Jesus fully realized all that was going to happen to him. Stepping forward to meet them he asked, 'Whom are you looking for?' 'Jesus of Nazareth,' they replied. 'I am he,' Jesus said. And as he said it, THEY ALL FELL BACKWARDS TO THE GROUND!" I almost tore Charles apart right on the plane yelling, "Look, look, look what it says in the Bible about falling under His power!" Once more God had let us see and taste of his supernatural power. (From our book, THE TWO SIDES OF A COIN).

My life has never been the same since that day when God's power went through my entire being. God knew the greatest need in my life, and He took this opportunity to do that miracle! It was not a healing miracle because I did not get healed of an eye problem. However, up until that time I had experienced every possible hang-up on the baptism with the Holy Spirit and speaking in tongues. God knew I needed this power, so in that split second of time when I yielded to His Holy Spirit, He took a spiritual eraser and removed from my mind every hang-up I had concerning speaking in tongues, and shortly after that, both Charles and I received this enduement of power.

Once we had tasted this supernatural touch of God and fallen under the power, we searched the scriptures to understand what additional information the Bible had concerning this phenomenon. We discovered terms such as "deep sleep"; "trance"; "as dead" describing "falling under the power".

Acts 9: 3-4   Speaking of Saul: *"And as he journeyed he came near Damascus, and suddenly a light shone around him from heaven. Then he FELL TO THE GROUND..."*

Acts 10:9, 10   *"Peter went up on the housetop to pray, about the sixth hour. Then he became very hungry and wanted to eat; but while they made ready, HE FELL INTO A TRANCE..."*

Acts 22:17   Paul speaking: *"Then it happened, when I returned to Jerusalem and was praying in the Temple, that I WAS IN A TRANCE and saw Him..."*

Rev. 1:17   *"...When I saw Him, I FELL AT HIS FEET AS DEAD."*

It was not long after I went under the power of God that Charles experienced this same supernatural touch from God. His life, like mine, has never been the same from the moment God personally touched him! Since that time God has let us see hundreds of thousands fall under the awesome power of the Spirit.

Many have asked over the years, "What good does it do?" When you have experienced this phenomenon, you will never be the same again because this is a divine touch upon your life placed there by the Almighty God! The transformed lives of individuals is the best testimony we know concerning this event.

How could we condense hundreds of thousands of testimonies into a few short words to let you see the glory of God from the beautiful experience of "falling under the power" or being "slain in the Spirit."

We are choosing one which you can multiply by as many thousands as you can imagine, and you will get a little concept of how much God will be doing in these last days when he touches great audiences, all at the same time.

This is a condensed story of David Fahey who worked for the railroad in Indianapolis, Indiana.

"First let me tell you that I am not a long-time Christian. I came from a non-Christian home, associated with non-Christian friends, participated in many non-Christian activities, and my attitudes throughout most of my life were also non-Christian.

"My wife, Karen, as a PK (preacher's kid) was involved deeply in church life and was trying to do what she thought was right. Suddenly she began to worry secretly about her salvation, and began reading the

Bible and bringing books home from the bookstore, like
GOD IS FABULOUS, HOT LINE TO HEAVEN,
HANG LOOSE WITH JESUS, all by a woman named
Frances Hunter.

"I thought she had flipped and one night she
calmly turned out the light and said, 'This Frances
Hunter lectures around the country and I would love to
go see her. Should she ever get to this part of the
country, will you take me?'

"'Sure honey, just let me know when. Fat chance,'
I thought. 'This Frances will never get to this part of the
country.' But not more than two weeks had passed
when Karen came running to me saying, 'Guess who is
coming to town next week!'

"I was expecting a few people to show up at the
basement of the Hilton meeting room, but was amazed
that the room was filled with about 400 people, all of
them with big smiles all over their faces, all of them
practically shouting, 'Hallelujah! Praise Jesus! Thank
you Jesus!' Words that I wasn't used to. I didn't
understand what was making them so happy, so I
started outside to smoke a cigarette and came to the
booktable. Everyone there was excitedly picking up
handfuls of books, and I saw two that Karen had
wanted so I bought them and went back to my seat in
the back row.

"They began singing when in walks Charles and
Frances Hunter, holding hands and shouting joy words
all the way to the front. I got the feeling that this was
not an ordinary author lecture. The first thing I knew an
unusual feeling came over me, and I was singing along
with them - songs about Jesus.

"I thought, 'Boy, I don't know what they have, but it can't be all bad if it makes you feel like they evidently feel.' Everyone was saying, 'Thank you Jesus, Praise you Jesus,' and to my amazement I was saying that too. I am even smiling! Suddenly I am aware that my hands are about to give me a fit. They are hot...they have turned a bright red. I cannot get them comfortable. I really don't know what to do with them. They are starting to make me nervous. What's the matter with my hands?'

"Just as quickly as the room became excited and noisy, it fell quiet. Frances stood quietly with her hands raised and her eyes closed. It was almost silent in the room. Then she began to speak, 'There are seven people in this room who are really having a most difficult time with their hands. They are uncomfortable, they are itchy and they are even feeling hot.'

"She was very calm, very matter-of-fact and very authoritative. I couldn't believe my ears. This woman, this complete stranger, this person that I had never seen before was telling me what my hands had been telling me for the past twenty-five minutes! I thought, 'This is not happening to me!'

"Frances continued, 'The Lord has a word for you seven people. Will you please come forward to receive it!

"Zzzzzap! A bolt of unseen lightning flashed out of nowhere and went down my spine sending a shower of sparks through every nerve in my body. Involuntarily I threw the books I had been holding on the floor and said, 'Oh my God!', and began to walk forward. It was as if a giant hand was pushing me from behind and I knew at once that if it was required of me that I would never look back even to say goodbye. There was no turning back for me. I know now that I was being irresistibly drawn to that which I had unknowingly been seeking for the better part of my life.

"Frances was talking again, her voice was soft with an almost 'cooing' quality about it. 'You seven people are chosen by the Lord for a great work. The Lord will anoint you this night and in due time you will become involved in and blessed with a healing ministry. Charles and I will now lay hands on you and pray the blessing of God upon you.'

"I quickly looked to my right and silently counted those who were standing with me. One, two, three, four, five, six, and myself - SEVEN! Not five, not ten, but seven just like she had said. How could this be? How did she know? How could it be that there were exactly seven people who came forward? There had been no confusion, no getting up and then sitting down by different ones. Just the seven who were in the front row now had stepped out and come forward.

"I was desperately trying to sort out what had been happening to me in the past thirty minutes when I looked up to see Charles' and Frances' hands reaching out to touch my head. They were both smiling, a smile that I have come to recognize in many people as the smile of Jesus Christ Himself.

"As they touched me I heard the now familiar words, "Thank you, Jesus, we love you, Jesus, we praise you, Jesus." ...and as the words seemed to fade away I felt myself becoming as light as a feather. Even as I unwillingly tried to keep my feet planted on the floor, I felt myself drift upward and then backward. A feeling so intense, so indescribably delicious began to consume me. It started deep within me at exactly I don't know where but I knew somehow without even the slightest molecule of doubt that what had been in my life before was being swept out. The empty spaces that were left from this sweeping were being filled with a wonderful warmth. A warmth that even though it is recognizable, it is indescribable.

"I was full! I was clean! I was really clean!

"Once again I began to see and hear what was happening around me in the room. My eyes had been closed and as I opened them I saw a hundred lights. I suddenly realized that it was a chandelier. I was flat on my back looking at the ceiling! With little effort I got to my feet and began to walk more than just a little unsteadily back to my seat. Karen whispered, 'What happened to you down there?'

"What had happened to me? I had fallen under the power of God. My life had really just begun.

"I went to work that night and came home the next morning and was taking a shower when an urge came to me like a flash. I needed to pray. What? Pray? Me pray? A voice within me said, 'Yes, pray as you have never prayed before.'

"There I was alone, dripping wet, and I thought to myself, 'What do I say?' Then it came to me...God had taken the time and trouble to pick me out of all those people, to put me on the floor and stir within me feelings and urges that I had never even heard of, let alone experience. I began to speak — out loud.

"'Father, though I do not understand all of this, I

know that it is of you and I therefore say that whatever you wish to do with me, then I shall accept it. Take my life, Father, take it if you will have it and I will serve you in any way and every way that I can, the best way that I can. I am sorry for all that I have done to displease you in the past and I will try to never make you unhappy or to hurt you again. I am all yours, Father. Please use me for your purpose and your glory.'

"At that moment Jesus Christ stepped into my life. I had asked Him and He had come just as I had always heard He would. Just think, I had been under the power of God *before* I was saved! Fantastic! Unbelievable! I was to discover it was just the beginning. I gave myself unconditionally to the Lord that Thursday morning. It was shortly after that when both Karen and I received the baptism with the Holy Spirit and our lives have been a thrilling delight since then. Just as Frances said, I have operated in the gifts of the Spirit, have led great numbers to Jesus and ministered the baptism with the Holy Spirit to them, healed the sick, cast out devils, and done the work of Jesus my Savior.

"Quite frankly, I am overwhelmed daily by the fact that in spite of my total unworthiness, my complete failure to come even close to that which He would have me be, God saw fit to reach down and touch me even before I had met Him through His Son Jesus Christ. He convicted me severely and completely, yet with such love and tenderness that I could no longer stand. In His infinite power He laid me prostrate and proceeded to cleanse me of the things of this world. Since I first got up off the floor and made my shaky way back to my seat, I have had a burning desire to get into His Word and to stay there until it is hidden in my heart.''

Can you even in your most far reaching imagination comprehend the magnitude of the work of this end generation that Jesus can do when great numbers of people fall under the awesome power of God and experience what David Fahey experienced? David has gone on to be a great leader among men in the Christian world. Multiply this by great hosts and see how Jesus will fulfill His requirement that *"This gospel of the kingdom will be preached in all the world as a witness to all the nations, and then the end will come"* (Matthew 24:14).

There have been times in our ministry when we have seen the multitudes fall out under the power of God with supernatural results. One such happening occurred in the state of Michigan at a campmeeting. We had ministered there for two nights previously and this was our final night.

Before the start of the evening service God spoke powerfully and said, "Minister to the children first." We contacted the State Superintendent who was in charge of the campmeeting and asked him if this was agreeable to him and he said it was.

We started the service about 6:30 in the evening with a short talk to the young people ranging in age from approximately six to eighteen. At the end of the talk we asked them ALL to say a sinner's prayer which they did. Then God spoke and said, "Go and lay hands on each and every one of them."

"And they brought young children to him, that he should touch them: and his disciples rebuked those that brought them. But when Jesus saw it, he was much

displeased, and said unto them, 'Suffer the little children to come unto me, and forbid them not: for of such is the kingdom of God''' (Mark 10:13, 14 KJV).

We stepped off the stage and laid hands on the first two children. They both fell under the power! We laid hands on two more children. They both also fell under the power! We laid hands on child number five and child number six, and they both also fell under the power, but none of them were getting up!

We continued walking through the tabernacle, and even outside on the grassy slopes, and the same thing happened to every child there except one! And they continued lying on the ground when *"suddenly there came a sound from heaven, as of a rushing mighty wind, and it filled the whole house where they were sitting. Then there appeared to them divided tongues, as of fire, and one sat upon each of them. And they were all filled with the Holy Spirit and began to speak with other tongues, as the Spirit gave them utterance"* (Acts 2:2-4).

It was as if they were all puppets and their bodies were controlled by strings because at a sound unheard by those in the audience, they ALL lifted their hands and began to speak with other tongues, as the Spirit gave them utterance! Many of these five hundred children were from Baptist, Methodist, Catholic and other evangelical denominations who had never heard of speaking in tongues, but the wind of the Spirit hit them all at the same time!

There was a hush that was so silent it could almost be heard as these five hundred children continued speaking in tongues with their hands lifted in the air.

A photographer was there from the Saginaw, Michigan, newspaper and he snapped numerous pictures all over the auditorium and seven full pages of pictures plus the story appeared in the Sunday newspaper! It was a night to remember, and we never go back to Michigan to minister but what someone reminds us of this most unusual night! We are still in touch with some of those young people, some of whom have gone on to graduate from Oral Roberts University with honors because they were completely transformed after a personal touch from God on that memorable night.

Three of the greatest times of the moving of the Spirit were in Canada; once in Nova Scotia, once in Saskatoon and once in Calgary. While there have been many, we have tried to select the three that were the most unique and unusual to us.

Our meeting in Nova Scotia was held in a basketball gymnasium, and on this particular night which had started out as many other services had, with worship and praise, the Lord directed us to minister in the area of fear. *"For God has not given us a spirit of fear, but of power and of love and of a sound mind"* (II Tim. 1:7). After teaching for approximately thirty to forty-five minutes, we asked anyone who wanted to be set free from a spirit of fear to come forward.

We were surprised to discover that over 800 people came forward to be set free! They were lined up all facing one direction when I began to break the power of the devil over them. Charles was standing at the front of the group, and I was on the stage at the approximate center of the group. As I used the powerful name of Jesus to break the evil spirit of fear, electricity could be felt in the air, and it was as though two tidal waves of power hit the people. One of the waves started in front of me as they *"ALL fell backwards to the ground!"* I turned to look at Charles at the head of the mass of humanity, and the second tidal wave had hit the front of the line as well and both waves simultaneously fell backwards to the ground. What a night of power! What a night of supernatural miracles. Charles ran back to the stage, and one lady came to him asking, "Where is my husband? I want to tell him that my blind eye is healed!" Many other testimonies of healings came forth as a result of this supernatural move of God's Spirit.

Someone said they could hear the wind blowing which sounded like a rising and falling sssssshhhhhhhhh, sssssssssssssshhhhhhhh, over the entire building as God swept over and touched all of those 800 individuals. Another person said it looked like waves of grain blowing in the wind!

One thing we know, it was a rushing mighty wind of the Holy Spirit that hit the people and every one of them went backwards under the power of the Spirit.

In Saskatoon, Saskatchewan we were ministering in a large church with pie-shaped sections of pews. This was the final night service and again God spoke to us to deal in the area of fear! After teaching on fear, we asked those who wanted to be delivered of a spirit of fear to raise their hands, and there was such a tremendous number, we noted quickly that we did not have enough room in the front to call them all forward at the same time, so we had the first section step out in the first aisle.

Charles and I left the pulpit and went down in the front of the first aisle and raised our hands and lightly touched one person on the forehead! Instantly it was as if someone had hit the entire group with a baseball bat, and they "ALL fell backwards to the ground!" It happened so quickly that all of us had to blink our eyes to see what had happened! Not only to see, but to believe that such a supernatural happening had actually occurred right in our midst!

As we moved to go to the second aisle, God spoke an unusual thought into my mind. He said, "There are those here who are full of unbelief and they think you pushed those people down. Return to the pulpit and tell them to watch for my glory and I will show them it is My mighty power which is doing this!"

We returned to the pulpit and shared with the audience what God had said, and we just stood there, waiting to see what God was going to do. There was an air of expectation and anticipation among many, and among others total unbelief that anything would happen! But happen it did!

It seemed supernaturally quiet for possibly sixty seconds, and then we heard a "thud".

The LAST two people in the line had fallen under the power of God!

Then came another "thud". The next-to-the-last two people in the line fell under the power of God. Then it seemed as though God hooked up a giant divine vacuum cleaner, and sucked every person in that section (approximately 200) down by a tremendous power, but each time he took those who were last in the line!

Before long, every single individual who had stood for deliverance from fear had been touched by the awesome power of God and was flat on the floor! A beautiful older lady of some 87 years said as she looked up at me from the floor, unable to get up because the divine pull was so strong, "I saw this kind of power back in 1905 and 1906, but I haven't seen it that way since!" Glory!

In Edmonton, Canada, at the great Jubilee Auditorium, we saw another example of this strange phenomenon which is not really strange at all when we understand that the Spirit of God is described as a mighty rushing wind, or breath. We can understand the term wind, but we can't really see it, nor can we see the wind of the Spirit; yet there is a similarity in the two.

One thing we do know is that we will see the mighty results of the wind of the Spirit more and more as we approach that grand day when we see Jesus split the clouds!

"The wind blows where it wishes, and you hear the sound of it, but cannot tell where it comes from and where it goes. So is everyone who is born of the Spirit" (John 3:8).

When we let God be God and do what He wants to do in our own lives we will see more and more of the supernatural. We were letting God have His way in Edmonton when more than two hundred people were instantly healed of arthritis in the audience! Suddenly, a divine command from God came to me. Again it was without a doubt in my mind that God was in control and was telling us what He wanted us to do to show His mighty power!

His words came into my brain with extreme clarity, loud and crisp. He said, "Tell the audience to watch my power and might! I will execute it in the center section only. Do not look to the right side. Do not look to the left side. Do not look in the balconies. Look only to the center section.''

I transmitted this divine information to the audience and then we waited in a Holy Spirit silence for the unexpected! Charles began to pray and as he did, the wind of the Spirit went in an oval swirl, similar to a whirlwind! About sixty people in the middle of the whirlwind fell under the power of God! Then the oval whirlwind enlarged and anyone inside of that heavenly elliptic fell under the power.

The intensity of the whirlwind increased and as it went faster and faster, more and more people fell out under the awesome power of the Almighty God until the wind disappeared, and in the center section there were only twelve people standing, and they were in the last row!

Not one person on the right side was touched!

Not one person on the left side was touched!

Not one person in either balcony was touched!

It was exactly as God had said. He specified only the center section, and nothing else, and that is exactly what happened! Someone asked me later why God only manifested Himself in the center section. Was He mad at the people in the other sections? I do not know why God picked the center section. I only know that He spoke it, and did it! And I don't ever question Him!

At a meeting sponsored by Marilyn Hickey Ministries in Greeley, Colorado, there was another explosion of God's power. Following is Marilyn's letter sent to us which appears in our book SINCE JESUS PASSED BY!

"Wally and I agreed that we had never been in such a service as the one in the ballroom of the Northern Colorado University at Greeley. You know, an hour before the doors were opened people were standing in the lobby singing worshipful choruses. We have been Assembly of God pastors for fifteen years and loved every moment of it, but I have never seen such a sovereign move of God as that night. As you are well aware when you both stepped on the platform and encouraged the people to join in a clap offering to the Lord (instead of for you), it appeared as though a clap of power hit the 1700 people. The first thing I heard was a thud. I looked up and to the left I saw a young woman who had fallen on the floor. Within a few moments a Lutheran girl I knew from the Study Retreats was on the floor behind her. Then suddenly all over the ballroom people had fallen out under the power of God. Some were laughing, some were praising, and speaking in tongues, some lay still and when we left at 11:30, there were still a few on the floor under the power of God in this way. *No human touched them.* We are still laughing with the joy of the Lord about those who were to come to the platform and testify of the healings they received and fell under the power as they started up the steps. I have no idea how many married couples came up to rededicate their married life to God and ended up on the floor. I laughed, I cried, I rejoiced and then suddenly I heard a thud and my husband was on the floor. He was there a long time, started to get up and fell back again and when he finally got back into his seat he was so drunk on the power of God, he hardly knew what was happening. He said it was like he had experienced the most relaxing time of his life and every bone was unhooked. That night will always be a memorial in my life — it showed me a new dimension of power. We have had people fall under the power in our services, we have seen some great moves of the Spirit in our church, but I have never seen such a sovereign move of God. Thank you, thank you for coming our way and giving of yourself so freely as channels for His power. Jesus is so irresistible and I am sure it would have been almost impossible to have resisted Him that night.

One of those who rededicated her life to Christ, received the baptism with the Holy Spirit and was completely 'zapped' by the power of God. She went straight home, gathered up $50.00 worth of ESP books and proceeded to burn them. Hallelujah!!!''

This was one of the most exciting nights of our whole life! Some 1700 jammed the ballroom for a miracle service. The power was so strong it was difficult to stand up. When the tremendous clap ovation for Jesus came, the power swooped down and somewhere around 200 people fell under the power right where they stood! The congregation was predominantly Lutheran and Catholic!

Then things really got exciting! The word
of knowledge started working and as we called
out healings, we asked them to come to the
platform and tell us what happened. Then we
made a startling discovery! The power of God
was so strong they couldn't get to the
microphone! We were both hanging on to the
pulpit because it was almost impossible for us
to stand. When anyone approached the
platform they looked like they had stepped on
a banana peel, and down they went, under the
power of God! A beautiful Catholic nun tried
to get to the mike, but instead fell on the floor,
personally touched by the hand of God! We
had written about this in our monthly
newsletter and today we received a letter which
said: "Yesterday I received another letter from
you where those approaching the platform
were not able to proceed, being overwhelmed
by the presence of God, and II Chronicles 7:2
tells of a similar encounter with God:

'And the priests could not enter into the
house of the Lord, because the glory of the
Lord had filled the Lord's house.'

Praise God that His glory can still fill the
temple! And praise God that His power has
not lessened one iota! "And when all the
children of Israel saw how the fire came down,
and the glory of the Lord upon the house, they
bowed themselves with their faces to the
ground upon the pavement, and worshipped,
and praised the Lord, saying, For he is good;

for his mercy endureth for ever." (II Chronicles 7:3 KJV).

If there is anything that will break down preconceived notions, beliefs, and ideas, it is watching or participating in a miracle service. God never seems to choose exactly the same way to do the same miracle. And often he does it in a humorous way. The following letter is self explanatory about an unusual way God worked in a couple's life!

"Dearest Beloved Frances and Charles.

"We want to share with you the miracle that has happened in our lives. The joyous miracle happened to my husband that Sunday night at the church in Tacoma. Dennis fell from a ladder (about 20 feet) while working in November 1972. He broke his knee in two places, also his heel. The doctors told him he'd never run again. He was left with a limp. Needless to say how hard it was for Dennis to accept this. Praise God.

At the service that night, Dennis was an UNBELIEVER all the way down the aisle. Matter of fact, the only reason he was going down that aisle with me was because of the 'couple' call. (You had invited couples forward to ask Jesus to bless marriages.) However, Praise the Lord, watching God's Holy Spirit move upon the people (starting to make him think) was scaring him to death, and confusion was in his mind all the way, until the final step was near, and we were next! He spoke with Charles first, to my surprise. Charles said to him, "What do you want Jesus to do for you?" Dennis said, "I hurt my knee falling off a roof last November and the doctors say I'll never be able to run again, and I want to run." Charles prayed a very short prayer and then said to Dennis, 'Now bend your knee,' and Dennis did, and discovered he could. Then Charles said, 'Now, RUN!' And Praise the Lord, God spoke through Charles to my husband. Like a bolt of lightning he started to run. Praise the Lord! Needless to say I'm left standing with Charles, and Charles didn't even know where he went. After a few minutes, here came my precious husband, sweating and crying, confessing and praying! I'm getting so excited writing this. Then another bolt of lightning! Both of us fell under the power with hands joined as one. The power of the Holy Spirit fell upon us, and oh, the glory of it all!

The joyous feeling that was in our 'one' heart as we left the church was wonderful. (Three months before this, we were planning a divorce.) Our marriage was on a solid rock called Jesus again after 12 years. Praise the Lord!

The second grand and glorious miracle that night, my husband pulled over to the side of the road a mile from home and said, 'Praise the Lord, I'll see you at home.' He started running like a deer through the night,

GLORY, GLORY, GLORY!!! I drove on home in amazement.

I've thanked Jesus many times for the pleasure of meeting and knowing another part of His family. You two will forever remain a part of our lives through Jesus Christ our LORD. In Jesus' name, thank you.

(signed) Connie and Dennis"

CHAPTER 15

SPECIAL ANOINTINGS
By Frances

"The Spirit of the Lord is upon Me,
Because He has ANOINTED Me to preach
*   the gospel to the poor.*
He has sent Me to heal the
*   brokenhearted,*
To preach deliverance to the captives
And recovery of sight to the blind,
To set at liberty those who are
*   oppressed,*
To preach the acceptable year of the
*   Lord"* (Luke 4:18, 19).

That special anointing the Spirit of the Lord had placed upon Jesus was transferred to us. *"But -- you hold a sacred appointment, you have been given an unction -- you have been ANOINTED by the Holy One, and you all know (the Truth)."* (I John 2:20 Amp.). *"But as for you, (the sacred appointment, the unction) the ANOINTING which you received from Him, abides (permanently) in you;..."* (I John 2:27 Amp.).

We can see that the anointing of the Holy Spirit is permanently with us because it is a gift from Jesus.

There comes at times a special supernatural outpouring of the Spirit which we often refer to as a special anointing. When this comes, it is a very precious time when God's power and presence is so upon us that most unusual manifestations of the Spirit are demonstrated.

Since these experiences were given to Jesus and to the disciples of the first generation, we know they will be given mightily in this last generation before His return.

"And the power of the Lord was present to heal them" (Luke 5:17). Apparently there were times in the life of Jesus while He was on earth that the anointing, the power, was greater than at other times.

One of the most anointed times in our ministry came very early in my public ministry. I recorded it in my book, IT'S SO SIMPLE (Formerly Hang Loose with Jesus).

NOT I, BUT CHRIST

One of the most unusual experiences of my entire life occurred when I had an opportunity to speak at a convention in June of 1969.

It all began like this. I had been at the same convention the year before autographing copies of my first book, *God Is Fabulous,* and had been real excited about being able to attend a large international religious convention (my first). I heard some inspired sermons, but somehow or other, I felt that something was missing in the campmeeting.

I felt led to pray upon returning home,

and this is what I prayed—I simply said: "Lord, they don't need to sit there and hear 18 sermons during the week. The lay people can hear sermons at home from their own pastor. What they need is something *new*—something to give them enthusiasm so they can return home *excited* about Jesus Christ, not with sermons to lull them into complacency about what good Christians they are. So, Lord, may I please have the opportunity of sharing the *excitement* I feel about Jesus Christ in that great auditorium so they'll wake up and go and tell the world the story of Jesus Christ?" I concluded with a "thank you" and then that prayer was recorded in the memory bank of my mind.

I probably was the least surprised person in the world when I received a letter stating that the committee was inviting me to speak on Thursday afternoon at 2:45 P.M. on the subject "Ways of Witnessing" — for the very simple reason that I had asked God to let me share my excitement about Jesus Christ, and certainly the reason I stay excited all the time is because I constantly witness as to the *now* power of God in daily living. There was probably nothing else in the letter that was earthshaking only some details to be followed, and that was all.

I immediately wrote back with great joy as follows: "My first reaction to speaking in that tremendous auditorium was violent

stomach pains, but then I remembered that
God has never called me to do anything that
He hasn't given me the ability to do, so it is
with great excitement and anticipation that I
accept the privilege of sharing the excitement I
feel in witnessing for Christ and in seeing souls
won for the army of Jesus Christ."

I had been on many speaking engage-
ments from the time I received the letter until
convention time, sharing the blessings of God.
Just before the convention I received a
memorandum telling what each speaker was
going to talk about and after my name was a
little notation, "I *think* she has chosen for her
subject, 'Go, Man, Go!'"

This was interesting, because somehow or
other, God has never led me to write out word
for word in advance what I'm going to share,
regardless of where I speak. I learned early in
my Christian life that God did not call me to
be a preacher, but instead just called me to
enthuse people, so my talking is constantly
sharing the things that Christ does in my life.

I may have even tried to prepare some
kind of a message for this *big* event, but
couldn't, and yet somehow or other, I knew
that God would give me the right words at just
the right time. (Please remember since I only
share what I have *seen* and *heard;* it is easy for
me to recall). I think it's interesting that everything we have ever seen, heard, felt, smelled or
touched is stored in a computerlike memory

bank of our mind and can be recalled at any time (not necessarily as *we* will it, but as *God* wills it).

I was excited about such a fabulous opportunity to share with people my ideas about "giving Christ away" and had no nervousness or apprehension (so I thought). The morning of my talk I got into the auditorium early and went up to the huge pulpit, which seemed about 20 feet above the ground, and looked out into the vast auditorium. I stepped back and then went back up there again and nearly fainted! It was huge!

I thought, "I'll never be able to do it!" Then I remembered the verse I had chosen. "I have been crucified with Christ; it is no longer I who live, but Christ who lives in me; and the life I now live in the flesh I live by faith in the Son of God, who loved me and gave himself for me." If I really believed this, how could I possibly be afraid, when it is Christ who is living his life through me. My usual exuberance returned and I spent the rest of the morning in a witnessing conference and then I ran over to my room to change clothes for the big event!

Maybe someone reading this book doesn't believe in the devil or the powers of Satan. Believe me, I do, because just about the time I got into the suit I had planned to wear, Satan started bombarding me. He said, "Who do you think *you* are, to get up in front of all those people and try to speak? What do you think you can say that will change their lives? You're just a layman. You're not a theologian or anything of the sort. Just wait until you see what a flop you're going to make of yourself." I could almost hear the fiendish laughter of Satan himself as he tried to put fear into my heart.

Something happened, and for the first time in my entire speaking life, I broke down and cried. I not only cried—I sobbed and sobbed as my whole body was convulsed with fear. I wanted to run as fast as I could—just anything to get away from that mammoth auditorium which looked like a huge mouth about to swallow me up. Then I remembered "I will *never* leave you, nor forsake you." (Heb. 13:5)

A cool breeze began blowing in the window and I felt like I was bathed in God's Holy Spirit, and two things happened simultaneously: A tremendous peace flooded my soul as I simply said, "God, with the power of your great and mighty Holy Spirit, I bind the hands of Satan, and claim victory for you this very day."

I didn't ask God to let me deliver the most powerful message or the greatest sermon or anything of the sort, but I very simply prayed with every fiber of my being and every ounce of sincerity I have in my body, "Lord, may your Holy Spirit walk in that great auditorium as He has never walked before." I blotted my tears, slipped into my shoes and walked directly to the auditorium. I wondered at that time if part of the letter to Ephesus wasn't written just for me in that year.

From the Phillips Translation, 1:15 it says (and I think of Paul talking directly to me): "Since, then, I heard of this faith of yours in the Lord Jesus and the practical way in which you are expressing it toward fellow Christians, I thank God continually for you and I never give up praying for you; and this is my prayer. That God, the God of our Lord Jesus Christ and the all-glorious Father will give you spiritual wisdom and the insight to know more of Him; that you may receive that inner illumination of the spirit which will make you realize how great is the hope to which He is calling you—the magnificence and splendor of the inheritance promised to Christians—*and how tremendous is the power available to us who believe in God. That power is the same divine energy which was demonstrated in Christ when he raised him from the dead* and gave him the place of supreme honor in Heaven."

Fear was gone because "perfect love castest out fear" and I was like a race horse running to the wire. All restraint was gone and there was nothing holding me back, and as I got up to speak, a most unusual feeling overcame me. Somehow or other, even though I was in a huge pulpit elevated high above the auditorium, I felt like I was sitting down on the stage, watching this person who had the same kind of white suit I had on, talk with absolute assurance about the things which God had done in her life.

As she shared story after story of different witnessing escapades, I knew somehow or other that they were mine—that they were things that had happened to me, and yet I sat right there listening to a voice which sounded just like mine spewing words out so fast I could hardly hear at times. I felt a tremendous urge to pray for this woman who looked like me, and sounded like me, because there was such an urgency in her voice, I wanted to ask God to make sure that she said everything that should be said, and then all of a sudden "I" was standing there.

I looked at my watch as this other woman was still talking and realized that my time was gone. My prayers, my dreams of God's Holy Spirit moving in a day-of-pentecost way, hinged on what this woman had said, and I realized that I had to listen to what "man" had said, because I must conclude by a certain time. I wondered, "Did God really hear my prayer this afternoon as I asked that His Holy Spirit walk in that auditorium as He had never walked before?" But I knew there was no more time. All the words that needed to be said were either said, or must now be left unsaid. Time had run out.

Emotionally I was drained, even though I felt like I had not been talking during the entire time, and I felt like crying, so I laid my head down on the pulpit and cried out, "God, hear my cry!" I don't even remember what I prayed because I was so overcome by the power of God that nothing seemed to matter. When I finished praying, I lifted my head, and the beautiful strains of "Kum Ba Ya" softly but completely enveloped the huge auditorium. Come by here, Lord! And come He did!

As I stood there it seemed to me everyone was getting up to go to conferences in groups of 50 at a time, and I wondered what had happened that so many people had to leave early to go to conferences, and then I got the shock of my life, because I realized they were not leaving, but responding to the power of God's Holy Spirit, and coming forward. The prayer rooms were filled in just a matter of seconds, and my pastor — who was sitting on the platform with me — stopped them from going in, and asked the people to stand in front of the huge platform.

For one brief moment, I believed that Satan tried his last fling because I might have thought "Wow, am I good!" but God cracked me right on the back of my knees and quietly but firmly said "Who did it, you or me?" I stepped back down from the pulpit, and never went up again because I knew that God had answered my prayer, but that nothing was to my personal credit. I remember looking out at all the people that God had touched — and I especially remember an old Negro standing there, with tears streaming down her face, but looking right up to Gloryland saying "Thank you, sir, thank you, sir!"

Praise the Lord that His Holy Spirit can work today to move people just like it did on the Day of Pentecost!

A few years later in a small town about three miles from where the special anointing came upon me, the anointing of the Spirit of God came upon Charles in a most unusual proportion.

So many fantastic things have happened to us since we accepted the baptism with the Holy Spirit that it could fill another book, just telling about the unusual services where God's power has moved in a tremendous way. We thought you might enjoy an article written following the first three services we had after publicly sharing about receiving the gift of the Holy Spirit. I wrote this the morning after it happened, sitting in a motel room on top of a box of books to put me high enough to use a typewriter I had borrowed. I called the article "Let's Take the Olive Oil Out of the Pulpit".

Thank you Jesus, for revealing such simple little truths to us all the time!

"Last night I sat in complete amazement as I listened to my own beloved husband, whose innermost thoughts are shared with me at all times, and heard and saw a completely different man. I saw a man so anointed by God that it was unbelievable. I don't believe there was anyone in the entire church who did not see the very special anointing of God upon his lips.

"He reminded me of a rushing river and all I could think of was 'Out of his innermost being shall flow RIVERS of living water.' And from out of his innermost being there poured the living water of Jesus Christ!

"On and on it came rushing forth as if he were powerless to stop, yet POWER-FULL enough to keep on going. Even though I was scheduled to be the speaker, I listened and realized that NOTHING should stop this tremendous surging tidal wave of the living water itself. It ran down into the valleys, it rolled across the rocky falls, and the power and the pressure of it smoothed the rough edges off of rocks and crags as it went racing through the channel that was Charles.

"For over one-and-a-half hours this went on, gaining momentum all the time. I happened to glance at the clock, and that's why I know how long it had been, and yet it seemed just like a few moments.

"I looked at the front pews of the church. Filled with young children from four to eight or nine years of age, they sat there completely under the spell of God's holy power. No wiggling, no squirming, no talking - just rapt attention. Nothing in the world except the power of God could ever keep little ones quiet that long.

"Charles apparently became aware of the time, but before he did, thoughts went flashing through my mind of 'what *short* talk can I give them tonight for my part of the service?'

"From the reservoir deep in my mind came all kinds of ideas and thoughts and experiences, but each one was wiped out instantly by the Holy Spirit. I began praying, 'Lord, what shall I share tonight to keep this flow going?' And each time another idea came into my mind, the Holy Spirit wiped it out again. Time went on and my mind raced faster and faster.

"I felt the pastor sit down in one of the chairs on the rostrum beside me. There was a gentle moving of air and a soft sound as he quietly sat down, but I didn't turn to look at him because I was so completely under the spell of the anointing of my husband. Finally after a minute or two, I felt a gentle tug on my sleeve.

"I turned to see what the pastor wanted and received the shock of my life! THE PASTOR WAS STILL SITTING DOWN ON THE FRONT PEW! I turned further to see who had sat down in the chair beside me and I'll never forget what I saw.

"I couldn't describe Him, other than the blue glow of an outline I saw, but I knew it was JESUS! He was sitting in the chair, legs crossed and arms on the arm rest of the chair. He said, 'Relax, the anointing is on Charles tonight. Let him have the entire service.'

"I ALMOST FELL OFF THE CHAIR!

"Cold chills ran up and down my spine as I realized that God was doing something very special in that church in Alexandria, Indiana that night!

"All of a sudden Charles temporarily dammed up the flow of living water and concluded with a remark similar to this: 'I must stop. You have asked Frances to speak. I must let her share what's on her heart.'

"And share I did! I only told them what had just happened up there on the rostrum of their church, and how Jesus had touched me and told me to keep silent. It was as though an electrical charge crackled through the entire congregation followed by a holy hush!

"It was a day of Pentecost! In the silence you could hear the rushing of the mighty wind of the Spirit. The 2,000 hours that Charles had spent in the Bible in one year, more than forty hours a week, came pouring out of him. The pastor said Charles stood there like another Paul who had spent time in the wilderness seeking Jesus in the Old Testament and who had found Him there. The torrent of words and revelations continued to pour from his lips.

"I was probably the most interested listener of all because out of his innermost being were flowing truths he had never discussed with me before. The extra hour he has been getting up and spending in the Bible daily from 5:30 until 6:30 every morning was pouring from his lips.

"God was blessing the prime time of his day which he had given to Him for the preceding three months. The constant searching for the spiritual meaning of God's Word had not been in vain. The lack of sleep had been more than repaid as God fulfilled His promise: 'Give, and it shall be given unto you.' The Lord gave back into his conscious mind all that he had stored in his subconscious, and had so anointed it that there was no one present who failed to feel the power.

"I had shared in both of the morning services because the Lord had not led us to feel he wanted Charles until the evening service.

"Both morning services had been anointed in a beautiful way, but they had only paved the way for the explosion of the Holy Spirit in the evening service. As we went to pray before the evening service, little realizing what was coming, the pastor said, 'Frances, you can't fail because of the way Charles prays for an anointing for you.' Then he asked Charles to pray for a special anointing at the night service, and Charles prayed for an 'explosion of the Holy Spirit' little realizing that he was praying for the anointing on himself.

"It was an explosion all right, but not the kind you might expect. It was quiet, but many said, 'It was the greatest service I have ever attended in my life.' Others said, 'It had to be the anointing of God, because Charles wasn't even aware of what was going on.' Many genuine decisions for Christ were made that night.

"Then another interesting thing occurred. Just the night before, some beautiful Spirit-filled men of the Full Gospel Businessmen's Fellowship had prayed for an anointing for Charles in this way, 'God, anoint him with the power of your Holy Spirit, with the *strength of Samson.*' And anoint him with that strength the Lord did!

"People called relatives as far away as Florida to let them listen to part of the tape far into the night and ran up and down the streets of Alexandria telling what had happened. God had called a church for something great! I had spoken in the morning about being a burning bush for the Lord and the first one at the altar was the song director who went to his own funeral as he completely died to self and gave all of himself to God. As we heard about him running up and down the streets sharing what had happened, in my mind's eye I could see him crying as in the days of Paul Revere, only instead of 'The British are Coming' it was 'Jesus is here!'

"There was one moment of real tension during the service, when I told Charles that Jesus had said the anointing was on him.

For a few moments the anointing left him as he looked at me in utter astonishment. I prayed silently in the Spirit with all the fervency I possessed for the anointing to return, and suddenly it was back upon him. The secretary of the church wrote me a letter the next day, which explains beautifully how a congregation lifted Charles up as they saw the anointing leave, and continued praying until the anointing returned.

"As Charles was speaking Sunday evening, it was so very evident that he had been anointed by God for a very special task. It had not been his intention to speak for the whole service but when Frances told him that she felt he should continue, there was a moment when he faltered ... and he was just Charles - not God's anointed one. My husband and I and our children were sitting in the fourth row and as Charles faltered there came upon us and over us wave after wave of the saints of the church holding Charles up again for the Spirit's anointing. As the first wave moved over Charles, the second wave moved over us and on and on until God had reanointed Charles for what God would have him to do. It was as though Charles was removed. His body only was there and we were hearing directly from God.

"You can imagine the excitement and peace and hush and precious spirit that was present! Praise the Lord for an unusual outpouring of His Holy Spirit!

"As I sat on the rostrum watching Charles, I saw a

bottle of olive oil obviously used for healing services and I had a perfect vision of what God had revealed to me a few short weeks before. When he admonishes us in James, *"Is any among you sick? Is any among you suffering? If so, let him call the elders of the church, ask them to anoint him with oil, and the prayer of faith will heal the sick,"* He *didn't mean olive oil at all!*

"All the way through the Old Testament, oil refers to the Holy Spirit, and when He said anoint the sick with oil, He meant to pray for the power of the Holy Spirit to touch the one who was suffering. He called those of us who believe and who are baptized with His Holy Spirit to lay our hands on the sick, and transmit to them by being nothing but a channel for Him, the beautiful healing power from on high. Right in front of my eyes I saw the two kinds of oil. The genuine, as it was being poured out all over Charles, and the substitute, sitting there with a cap on the top, all bottled up.

"The difference between success and failure.

"The difference between churchianity and Christianity.

"The difference between God and man.

"It is God himself, in his mercy, who has given us (Charles and Frances) *this wonderful work (of telling his Good News to others), and so we never give up. We do not try to trick people into believing - we are not interested in fooling anyone. We never try to get anyone to believe that the Bible teaches what it doesn't. All such shameful methods we forego. We stand in the presence of God as we speak and so we tell the truth, as all who know us will agree.*

"If the Good News we preach is hidden to anyone, it is hidden from the one who is on the road to eternal

death. Satan, who is the god of this evil world, has made him blind, unable to see the glorious light of the Gospel that is shining upon him, or to understand the amazing message we preach about the glory of Christ, who is God. We don't go around preaching about ourselves, but about Christ Jesus as Lord. All we say of ourselves is that we are your slaves because of what Jesus has done for us. For God, who said, 'Let there be light in the darkness,' has made us understand that it is the brightness of his glory that is seen in the face of Jesus Christ.

"But this precious treasure - this light and power that now shine within us - is held in a perishable container, that is, in our weak bodies. EVERYONE CAN SEE THAT THE GLORIOUS POWER WITHIN MUST BE FROM GOD AND IS NOT OUR OWN" (2 Corinthians 4:1-7 TLB).

Jesus appeared to the disciples of the early church, and we know He will appear to many of His disciples in this final chapter before His arrival to usher us into heaven!

CHAPTER 16

ANGEL VISITATIONS
By Charles & Frances

Charles:
Will angels be visible to more of the Body of Christ in the end church than in the early church? About a third of all mention of angels in the Bible is in the book of Revelation, and we believe that is the day in which we are living now!

Since we wrote the great soul-winning book, ANGELS ON ASSIGNMENT, we have had hundreds of people come to us with testimonies of seeing angels or having had visits by angels. The exciting thing about some of these witnesses is that we have seen the angels appear in the same place they tell of seeing them, and they describe the angels as we have seen them. God does confirm his Word by many witnesses.

The first known direct visit from angels in our lives came on the night of my birth. My mother didn't tell me about this until late in her life, after God had placed us in a miracle ministry. She said that angels appeared at her bedside, handed her a little package and said, "This is your beloved son!'' Then the angels vanished.

Soon after we received the baptism with the Holy Spirit, we were ministering in a miracle service in Austin, Texas. Frances and I, the worship leader and another man were on the stage of the auditorium. During the beautiful worship, Frances turned to the worship leader and said, "Will you lead us in singing in the Spirit?" He looked rather shocked that she would make such an earthly request for such a heavenly act as singing in the Spirit, but Paul said he sang with the Spirit, so why shouldn't we?

Just before the worship leader started to sing in tongues, we both turned toward the piano.

Coming from that direction we heard what sounded like a thousand piece orchestra tuning their instruments just before a concert. But ... the piano bench was empty and a guitar was resting beside the bench! The volume began to intensify as they seemed ready for the down-beat of the orchestra leader, when simultaneously with the worship leader starting to sing in the Spirit, the whole invisible orchestra played in harmony with this beautiful singing in tongues. What an awesome experience for us and the worship leader as we heard the music of a thousand angels!

Frances:

Years later in Montana we were speaking in a convention held in a huge tent where about 700 Spirit-filled people were in attendance. We had just shared the powerful story from the message brought by Gabriel as told in the chapters, "He Tasted Death" and "You Are Covered (Atonement)" in the book, ANGELS ON ASSIGNMENT. Nothing brings the glory of God like magnifying Jesus through His sacrifice and His blood offering to God.

As Charles finished sharing this beautiful atonement message, I stepped to the microphone. Instead of ministering healing which we usually did at that time, I began singing in the Spirit and the voices of 700 people joined in the beautiful worship as though it was a unified thanks to God for sending Jesus to us. The volume swelled in harmony and it was the most beautiful singing we had ever heard.

Then it seemed that everyone began to listen and look up as they were worshiping. This continued for several minutes and nobody wanted to stop. Suddenly it ended in a holy hush!

God spoke in prophecy and said, "Because of your adoration and praise of me this night, I have sent a heavenly host from the other side to join you in praise and worship!"

What we saw and heard was a spectacular display of God's glory. There were more worship angels than there were people, the angels hovering near the top of the giant tent, and for the first time in my life, I heard them singing. They sounded like high pitched violins but were singing in angel languages! Glory to God!

Then came the final thrill when people came running to us after the service saying, "Did you see the angels and hear them singing with us when we were singing in tongues?" Each description was alike, and then they said, "When they finally left, a heavenly mist descended from the top of the tent."

We are living in the most exciting age of all times! Hallelujah!

We love to worship God and Christ Jesus and in each of our miracle services we spend a lot of time in praise and worship. Generally the congregation will break into praise in the Spirit as they sing with their spirits like Paul did.

It was on one such occasion in a morning service in the Abilene, Texas Civic Center that the sponsoring pastor, Wilson Estes, came to us and was unusually excited with what he had just seen and experienced.

He said he was in high worship when he looked toward the stage and all across the top of the stage valance he saw a row of small angels. He continued to praise God, singing in the Spirit, and looked again. This time there were two rows of angels; in back of the row he first saw was a row of large warrior angels.

He said, "God, what does this mean?"

God said, "The first row are worship angels I have sent to join you in worship and praise. The second row are warrior angels I have sent to fight the spirit of religiosity which is over Abilene."

We looked all over, above, and around the stage but we could see nothing that looked like an angel!

We asked Pastor Estes to share about the angels in the evening service. When he finished, I began to prophesy about what God was going to do in Abilene, and when I finished, Charles stepped to the microphone to speak, when suddenly I was aware of the fact that there was someone on the stage with us. In my spirit I knew it was an unusual person, but I had no idea what it really was, so I began to step back very slowly, very slowly, so that I could be in line with the person who was standing there. Somehow I knew it was not God or Jesus, but I knew it was some type of heavenly being, so I continued moving slowly backwards so I could see who it was because I didn't want to disturb the meeting, when suddenly I turned, and there STOOD THE BIGGEST MAN I'VE EVER SEEN IN MY ENTIRE LIFE. Instantly I knew it was an angel! And at the top of my lungs (not wanting to disturb the meeting) I said "WOW!" What a moment of Glory!

He was approximately eight feet tall and he had the biggest shoulders I've ever seen in all my life. I was so completely overcome with the presence of this angel that I could not say a single word! Then God spoke to my heart and said, "That's a special warrior angel that I have stationed with you and Charles to protect you from the fiery darts of the devil until Jesus Christ comes back!"

Those words are burned into my very heart, and even as I write this, I can hear them again! The thing that excited me so much was the last five words "until Jesus Christ comes back!" Hallelujah! Surely we are in the very end times!

I have seen the angel many times since then, and am always aware of his presence whether we are on a plane or in a car, and what a comfort to know that he's protecting us at all times from the fiery darts of the devil!
Charles:
We were to be guests and participate in a wedding one Sunday evening. It was about an hour before the church service and time for the wedding to start when a man brought his badly crippled wife into the foyer of the church. We ministered healing to her, but God put her in traction to heal her back, and it took about ten minutes for the total healing to be accomplished. The

groom got very nervous, but we said God wanted to finish the miracle. She was totally healed after months of excruciating pain.

While the minister was conducting the wedding, I asked him if I could interrupt for a moment. The bride and groom were facing us as we faced the audience. I told the audience that this was an unusual wedding because the giant angel whom God had stationed with us was standing directly in back of the bride and groom, facing us. Then I said he was moving to my right; then he was moving back to Frances.

I have never seen this angel or any of the large angels, but God gives me an ability in the Spirit to tell exactly where the angel is and know his movements without visibly seeing him. Frances then took the microphone and said, "Charles described him perfectly (she saw him as plainly as she could see me), except that when he moved to our right, he put his hand on the shoulder of the man sitting there. The man accepted Jesus that night after the wedding!"

One night we were worshiping in a church in Kalamazoo, Michigan, and I nudged Frances as we were leading the worship, and said, "Do you see the angels?" We were worshiping Jesus and the worship angels appeared in cluster-like groups of five or six. They were joyously clapping their hands in blissful praise. They looked very excited as they were worshiping Jesus whom they love so very much, and honor so respectfully.

The worship angels seem to be about four or five feet high, while big warrior angels seem to range from about seven to eight feet tall.

One night in Massachusetts on the last night of a

three-day seminar, we had urged the people to go out into their part of the world and minister salvation to the people who don't know Jesus. Frances suddenly stopped talking and began telling what she saw in amazement. Standing in military-like formation, shoulder to shoulder along both sides and across the back of the auditorium were about a hundred giant angels dressed like warriors. God gave her a prophecy message for the people: "Don't be afraid to tell about Jesus and the Gospel, because when you are doing this you will never be alone. I will send one of these giant angels with you!"

Twelve people came to us after the service and each of them described the angels alike in more detail than Frances had related over the microphone.

When Pastor Buck (ANGELS ON AS-SIGNMENT) related about seeing about a hundred giant warrior angels standing on his lawn in front of his house, we believed. This special visit from heaven gave us a personal confirmation of one of the mighty sights Pastor Buck related to us as we wrote the book which has led over a quarter of a million people to Jesus.

CHAPTER 17

FIRE FROM HEAVEN
By Frances

If it happened in Bible times, it will happen today!
"The year King Uzziah died I saw the Lord! He was sitting on a lofty throne, and the Temple was filled with his glory. Hovering about him were mighty, six-winged seraphs. With two of their wings they covered their faces; with two others they covered their feet, and with two they flew. In a great antiphonal chorus they sang, 'Holy, holy, holy is the Lord of Hosts; the whole earth is filled with his glory.'

"Such singing it was! It shook the Temple to its foundations, and suddenly the entire sanctuary was filled with smoke.

"Then I said, 'My doom is sealed, for I am a foul-mouthed sinner, a member of a sinful, foul-mouthed race; and I have looked upon the King, the Lord of heaven's armies.

"Then one of the seraphs flew over to the altar and with a pair of tongs picked out a burning coal. He touched my lips with it and said, 'Now you are pro-

nounced 'Not guilty' because this coal has touched your
lips. Your sins are all forgiven.'

"*Then I heard the Lord asking, 'Whom shall I send*
as a messenger to my people? Who will go?'

"*And I said, 'Lord, I'll go! Send me'*" (Isaiah
6:1-8 TLB).

God continually confirms his Word with signs and
wonders, and so often he does some of the most unusual
things.

Tuesday night, January 29, 1979, was a night we
will never forget. It all started as Charles and I read the
confession from A CONFESSION A DAY KEEPS
THE DEVIL AWAY. "Thank you, Father, that angels
are in charge of me. I am surrounded by angels at all
times who minister to me and protect me, even from
accidents. I am accompanied by angels, defended by
them and preserved by them because you have ordered
them to do so." (Reference: Psalm 91:11)

We were sitting in the restaurant as I read this, and
as soon as I finished, God spoke and said, "TONIGHT
THERE WILL BE A VISITATION OF ANGELS IN
THE CHURCH!"

I almost fell off of my chair.

I shared this in the morning session, and the
organist spoke up and said, "Last night I felt the
presence of an angel on the front pew, but I couldn't see
him, and asked God to please let me see him, but he
said, 'Not tonight, but tomorrow night.'"

What a confirmation!

The pastor of the church immediately jumped to
his feet and said, "I want to share something I've never
shared before." Then he shared a story of how he heard

the angels sing the night he was saved 60 years before. He was baptized with the Holy Spirit at the same time, but he had never heard the angels sing again, and had asked God the previous week to let him hear the angels once more. Just seven or eight days prior to our being in the church, God let him hear the angels sing again.

More confirmation!

There was a great excitement at the start of the evening meeting, and an awareness of the presence of God in an unusual way. A prophecy came forth from another of the pastors saying that fire would come down from heaven that very night. The excitement mounted!

We worshipped, we taught, we preached the Gospel, and still we saw nothing of the angels God said would be there. We talked on total commitment of our lives and holy living that evening and asked all who wanted to release their lives totally to God and die to self to stand and come forward. The front of the church was filled, the aisles were filled all the way to the back of the church, because God had touched the hearts of the people.

Suddenly I saw an angel appear in the back of the church. He was blowing a trumpet, apparently sounding a call for other angels.

This all happened as the crowd surged forward, and along with them came other angels which had appeared right after the trumpet call. Each angel had one coal of fire held in a small pair of tongs. As they came over the crowd, each angel proceeded to place the coal of fire on the lips of individuals throughout the standing congregation.

As I saw each angel descend to leave the coal, I

went to that person and touched their lips and unusual things happened! One of the pastors said he never felt such power in his life, and when I touched his lips he wondered if I had actually hit him in the mouth. He went under the power and while he was on the floor, he reached up to see if his lips were bleeding because he felt such a breath of power!

A young man who received a coal of fire had not received the baptism with the Holy Spirit, and as soon as I touched his lips he fell under the power and began to speak in tongues.

Some did not receive coals, and Charles received a word of prophecy. God said that there was a wall or blockage holding some of them back from receiving a special anointing. He said it in great love, not being judgmental, and the message continued that they would be awakened between two and three o'clock in the morning by the Holy Spirit!

And they were! The next night a couple came in with nine packs of cigarettes. She said the presence of God was so real the night before she began to weep because she was afraid she wouldn't make it to heaven and God said, "I want your cigarettes." Both she and her husband turned in their cigarettes, completely delivered because of this unusual visitation.

A young man who had stolen a diamond ring, confessed that he had swallowed it when the police examined him, but that it had later been stolen from him, and the convicting power of the Holy Spirit was so strong that he heard God say, "You still owe the jeweler for that ring, even if it was stolen from you." He said he was going to make a restitution, and people began giving money to help him make the restitution.

At two-thirty in the morning, a woman was awakened and heard one word, "Miriam." On Wednesday night, we shared the story of Miriam and Aaron talking and gossiping behind Moses' back, and envying God's treatment of him, and this woman confessed her envy of someone else in the congregation because of their talents. (Read Numbers, Chapter 12).

However, the most exciting testimony came from the pastor himself. He said, "I didn't see any angels, I didn't feel a thing when Frances placed her hands on my lips, but I preached all night long. I preached in my sleep, I preached when I was awake, and folks, you've got a brand new pastor." The anointing on him was tremendous.

We don't understand everything about angels, but how we praise God for the ministering work performed by the angels that night!

We really didn't know that there was a similar story in the Bible until one day we were reading and discovered the story as quoted above in Isaiah Chapter six.

We still wonder what God meant, but as we look back to the age God talked about in the rest of that chapter when Israel was scattered, and now look at this end generation when the Jews have again become a nation, could this mean that we disciples who are to be used to go tell the world about the cleansing power of God will be the totally committed people whose only desire is to say, "Lord, I'll go! Send me."

"Now when the Day of Pentecost had fully come, they were all with one accord in one place. And

suddenly there came a sound from heaven, as of a rushing mighty wind, and it filled the whole house where they were sitting. Then there appeared to them DIVIDED TONGUES, AS OF FIRE, and one sat upon each of them. And they were all filled with the Holy Spirit and began to speak with other tongues, as the Spirit gave them utterance" (Acts 2:1-4).

Charles:

We had almost completed writing the great book ANGELS ON ASSIGNMENT, and were in an afternoon service in a church in Wycoff, New Jersey. I was telling the congregation about God stationing the angel with us to protect us from the fiery darts of Satan until Jesus Christ comes back; about many of the exciting visits of Gabriel and the other angels to Pastor Buck, and about some of the messages God sent to us, the Body, by the Angel Gabriel. I was bubbling over with excitement about this when suddenly one whole row of people jumped to their feet and began pointing toward us and shouting, "Look behind you, look behind you! Shafts of light! Shafts of light!" Others began popping up all over the church shouting the same thing and pointing toward us.

We could have kicked ourselves for not immediately looking, but as they were shouting, I felt a force of energy pouring into my body from behind my left shoulder like from a fire hose. It seemed to penetrate my whole body and I have never felt such a powerful presence or flow of the power of God in my life. Frances and I were standing behind a large pulpit side by side when the power of the Holy Spirit came down on us like ten thousand pounds of glory and we both slumped over on the pulpit.

This power felt much like the gravity pull on a plane which speeds in a steep climb upwards, but only in reverse. It was the power of God that pushed us down on the pulpit.

After this visitation ended, we talked to the congregation saying we did not know what this was, but reminded them of some similar visits in the Bible.

For example, in Exodus 3:2-8: *"And the Angel of the Lord appeared to him in a flame of fire from the midst of a bush. So he looked, and behold, the bush burned with fire, but the bush was not consumed ... (8) So I have come down to deliver them out of the hand of the Egyptians, and to bring them up from that land to a good and large land, to a land flowing with milk and honey ..."*

In this end generation, God is again visiting earth with His angels with the message of deliverance. So much of God's end-time messages in the book ANGELS ON ASSIGNMENT relate to His deliverance of His people by the cleansing blood of Jesus. God never ceases to reach His big arms of love out to those who are not serving Him, always wanting them to come to Him and be His children. His love is everlasting and is being poured out so freely in this generation, wanting none to perish!

We also called their attention to Acts 9:3-6: *"And as he* (Saul) *journeyed he came near Damascus, and suddenly a light shone around him from heaven. Then he fell to the ground, and heard a voice saying to him, 'Saul, Saul, why are you persecuting Me?' And he said, 'Who are You, Lord?' And the Lord said, 'I am Jesus, whom you are persecuting. It is hard for you to kick against the goads.'*

"So he, trembling and astonished, said, 'Lord, *what do You want me to do?' And the Lord said to him, 'Arise and go into the city, and you will be told what you must do.'"*

That was one of the most awesome experiences of my life, but we still didn't know what this special visitation was until we were with Pastor Buck to whom God had sent the angels so many times. I asked Pastor Buck to tell us some of the messages and visits which he had not yet shared with us. He said, "I don't believe I told you, but Gabriel and Chrioni came to my study one night and said to tell Charles and Frances that they had dropped in on some of their services, but to tell them that they did not appear as they usually do, but appeared AS SHAFTS OF LIGHT!"

Glory to God! Gabriel is the angel who stands nearest to God (Luke 1:19) and this radiation of the presence of God on him was what I felt so strongly that afternoon!

As we have shared what God is doing and will be doing to accomplish those "greater things" Jesus said we would be doing, He has given us confirmations along the way, building our faith to move into new dimensions of His power and glory.

We were sharing this end-time message in Saskatoon, Saskatchewan, Canada when I suddenly stopped sharing, and said, "I have never felt the radiating power of God so strong as I do right now except the time when Gabriel stood behind us in New Jersey."

The next night a young lady who had been saved

only about two months came with the people who came to the hotel to take us to the meeting. She was so excited because she wanted to tell us what she saw the night before while we were sharing this story of God's glory. She said there appeared a large angel, about eight feet high, and he was pacing back and forth behind Frances and me. She said he would walk up behind us and put his hands on both our shoulders, then he would walk some more, and then come to first one of us and then the other and lay his hands on our shoulders. Hallelujah!

She said that as she was watching this big angel, something like a cloud of thin smoke filled the top of the auditorium and she began looking at this cloud when there appeared hundreds of little angels in the cloud. We often see this cloud of glory fill the temple when we are worshipping God and Jesus and during miracle services. Many times we have seen God's worship angels appear in this cloud of glory just like this young girl described.

We know this was a different angel than the one God stationed with us because when "our" angel is near us we do not feel this radiating power; we are aware of his presence and often Frances sees him physically appear in her spirit vision. Pastor Buck related that this power emanating out of Gabriel and the other angel with him was so strong one time that he started falling down the stairs, but the angels caught him and strength came back into him. He said that when an angel stays on earth for long periods of time, this power fades like the glory of God faded from the face of Moses after he came down from the mountain after having been with

God.

We believe this appearance of a heavenly being was another of the many confirmations God is giving that this message of the greater things He wants to do through the Body of Christ is from Him and is for us today.

CHAPTER 18

GOD'S GLORY
By Charles and Frances

God has displayed His Glory in multitudes of ways throughout all ages of this earth.

The rainbow of promise from God to His creation is spread across the sky as a showcase of His beautiful glory. All people of all ages since the first rainbow was ever placed in the sky by God have watched His glory exhibited with a feeling produced by something majestic, sublime, beautiful, awesome! We recognize God in His creation!

When we see the sky filled with lightning flashes, and hear the thunder of his power we stand in awe! God is reminding us of His power and His glory!

When we see the wonders of the color, the variety, the created beauty of His flowers and vegetations placed upon this earth for the pleasure of His people, we see the glory of God paraded before our very eyes. God shows off for His people, and we are blessed to be His people! Oh, how much love and tender care and concern He has for all of us, even for those who do not love Him back.

"For God so loved the world that He gave His only begotten Son, that whoever believes in Him should not perish but have everlasting life" (John 3:16). God presented His greatest beauty, His greatest love before us as He sent His royal Son to become one of us so that we could be one of His royalty.

What a mighty God we serve. Why would anyone not want to release total control of their lives into the loving hands of such a God as He?

We know of no greater way to describe God and His glory than to go directly to His Word. As we look at the description God gave of Himself and His works and power in Job, chapters 38 and 39, we see evidence of His greatness.

But even as we see His creation, His goodness to us, we can only finally get a glimpse of His glory when we read what Jesus said to His Father, to our Father, in the seventeenth chapter of John. Because it is so beautifully paraphrased in The Living Bible, we want you to read it again as we have, and see God's glory!

"When Jesus had finished saying all these things he looked up to heaven and said, 'Father, the time has come. Reveal the GLORY of your Son so that he can give the GLORY back to you. For you have given him authority over every man and woman in all the earth. He gives eternal life to each one you have given him. And this is the way to have eternal life--by knowing you, the only true God, and Jesus Christ, the one you sent to earth! I brought GLORY to you here on earth by doing everything you told me to. And now, Father, reveal my GLORY as I stand in your presence, the GLORY we shared before the world began.

"'I have told these men all about you. They were in the world, but then you gave them to me. Actually, they were always yours, and you gave them to me; and they have obeyed you. Now they know that everything I have is a gift from you, for I have passed on to them the commands you gave me; and they accepted them and know of a certainty that I came down to earth from you, and they believe you sent me.

"'My plea is not for the world but for those you have given me because they belong to you. And all of them, since they are mine, belong to you; and you have given them back to me with everything else of yours, and so THEY ARE MY GLORY! Now I am leaving the world, and leaving them behind, and coming to you. Holy Father, keep them in your own care -- all those you have given me -- so that they will be united just as we are, with none missing. During my time here I have kept safe within your family all of these you gave me. I guarded them so that not one perished, except the son of hell, as the Scriptures foretold.

"'And now I am coming to you. I have told them many things while I was with them so that they would be filled with my joy. I have given them your commands. And the world hates them because they don't fit in with it, just as I don't. I'm not asking you to take them out of the world, but to keep them safe from Satan's power. They are not part of this world any more than I am. Make them pure and holy through teaching them your words of truth. As you sent me into the world, I am sending them into the world, and I consecrate myself to meet their need for growth in truth and holiness.

"'I am not praying for these alone but also for the

future believers who will come to me because of the testimony of these. My prayer for all of them is that they will be of one heart and mind, just as you and I are, Father -- that just as you are in me and I am in you, so they will be in us, and the world will believe you sent me.

"'I have given them the GLORY you gave me -- the GLORIOUS unity of being one, as we are -- I in them and you in me, all being perfected into one -- so that the world will know you sent me and will understand that you love them as much as you love me. Father, I want them with me -- these you've given me -- so that they can see my GLORY. You gave me the GLORY because you loved me before the world began!

"'O righteous Father, the world doesn't know you, but I do; and these disciples know you sent me. And I have revealed you to them, and will keep on revealing you so that the mighty love you have for me may be in them, and I in them.'"

Probably the greatest earthly glory ever seen is in the miracle of the birth of a child. When God created man and woman and gave this ability for the man to plant a seed containing a human life into the womb of a woman, He was displaying his glory in creation.

The very greatest glory ever seen on earth was when Jesus came to earth as a human being. Then God continued displaying His glory by placing a portion of Himself into the spirit of man when His seed, His sperm, His life is planted into the spirit of man - His seed being Jesus. When we are born again by the Spirit of God, we actually do have Jesus, the seed, the life of God, in us. That is truly the greatest miracle we will ever see on earth, and that is God's glory.

CHAPTER 19

THE PLOWMAN
SHALL OVERTAKE THE REAPER
By Frances

"Behold, the days are coming," says the Lord,
"When the plowman shall overtake the reaper,
And the treader of grapes him who sows seed;
The mountains shall drip with sweet wine,
And all the hills shall flow with it.
I will bring back the captives of My people Israel;
They shall build the waste cities and inhabit them;
They shall plant vineyards and drink wine from them;
They shall also make gardens and eat fruit from them.
I will plant them in their land,
And no longer shall they be pulled up
From the land I have given them."
Says the Lord your God (Amos 9:13-15).

As we were describing the various and unique ways God has been dealing with us in the area of the "greater" things, Alan Jandl, who pastors the great Living Stones Church in Alvin, Texas, shared that scripture with us and the explanation given in his book SEND THE WORD!

He said that God had awakened him at 5 o'clock one morning and began to deal with him concerning the rapid increase that is going to take place according to His Word. He said, "I read that first verse over and over. Finally, way down inside of me, I began to see a man sowing grape seeds. As soon as they hit the ground, immediately a vine would grow and grapes would form, and a man would pick them, put them in a trough and tread out those grapes. That is a supernaturally fast rate -- to plant and have God instantly add the increase."

And when is that day going to be? The rest of the scripture tells us that it will occur when the mountains shall drip with sweet wine, and today grape vineyards cover the former wastelands of Israel. God said that He would bring back the captives of Israel who would then rebuild their cities and inhabit them. This is happening today in Israel.

Israel became a nation in 1944 and raised their flag in 1948 and they have been making gardens and eating fruit from them. Today Israel is raising more fruit per square foot of ground than any other nation in the world. And God has promised that Israel shall never be pulled up again from their land.

The time for the supernaturally natural fast rate with an instant increase before the seed even goes into the ground is RIGHT NOW because all of the rest of the things which were mentioned in that scripture have been fulfilled!

Visualize in your spirit, if you can, the supernatural growth of a grape seed dropped into the ground and its maturity within the twinkling of an eye, almost before it hits the ground, and then visualize the miraculous power of God accelerating and accomplishing the same things in salvation, baptism with the Holy Spirit, healings and deliverance.

Visualize one word spoken, and salvation received!

Visualize one hand waved over the multitudes, and see them all healed by the power of a loving God ... instantly!

Visualize instantaneous deliverance of hundreds of thousands of demon-possessed or oppressed people!

When is this going to happen? Today -- right now, if we will learn that fine tuning that is necessary to be able to operate in those things which the Holy Spirit is trying to communicate to us!

On a trip to the midwest, we had rented a car and were turning it back in at an off-the-airport lot. Once the papers have been returned to the rental car agency, it has to be driven by one of their regular employees, so Charles slipped into the back seat while a young man climbed into the front seat to take us on the three-minute drive to the airport.

On the back of his T-shirt were the words, "Success is ..." and the rest we didn't see well enough to read. Charles said, "Did you know that Jesus always promises success?"

The young man said, "No, I never heard of anything like that!"

I said, "Did anyone ever tell you that Jesus Christ is the most exciting man who ever lived, and that church is the most fabulous place in the world to go to have excitement in your life?"

He turned sideways to look at me and said, "Nobody ever told me anything like that!" And I could see that in his mind he was thinking that was the wildest statement he had ever heard in his entire life!

Charles entered the conversation again and said, "He never provides for failure, only success, and along with that, He gives you peace in your heart, joy and a purpose for living!"

The young man, obviously stunned by this time, was turning into the airport and he said, "He will?"

Charles said, "Yes, he will. Would you like to ask him to forgive your sins and come into your heart?"

The young man instantly said, "You bet I would!" And before we had reached the airline on which we were going out, he had prayed the sinner's prayer, we had instructed him about getting into an exciting church, I was scribbling down the name and address of the church from which we had just come, and He was saying, "I'm going to go to church. I'm going to start reading the Bible, just like you said!"

He carried our luggage into the airport for us, and with tears in his eyes walked away, a new creature in Christ! Almost before the seed was dropped into the fertile ground, it came up, full-blown!

Somewhere along the line, we know that someone else sowed, someone else watered, but now is the time for us to put in the sickle and harvest the crop!

On this same trip as we returned to Houston, Charles motioned to an aircap that we would need him as soon as the luggage came down, and in the approximate time span of no more than two minutes maximum, Charles said, "Do you know Jesus?"

The aircap said, "No, sir!"

Charles said, "Would you like to?"

The aircap said, "Yes, I would!" and prayed the sinner's prayer!

You might think this type of salvation could not possibly work -- or last even if it did work momentarily. We have seen this same aircap several times since then, including one week after he prayed the prayer. He saw us coming, grabbed our luggage and said, "I'm the one who prayed that prayer last week, and it's changed my life!" A few weeks later he again came running up to us and said, "Thank you, thank you, thank you for what you did to my life!" And every time we see him he reminds us of something that Jesus has done in his life! This is end-time harvesting!

During a meeting in St. Louis at the Life Christian Center, a woman was so convicted by the power of the Holy Spirit, that she could not wait until the end of the service for salvation and broke out and came running up. Her son came also, and he accepted Jesus at the same time! People come up to us during services and are crying, "I want to get saved!" This is God pouring out of His Spirit in these last days!

At Billy Joe Daugherty's church which meets at the Mabee Center in Tulsa, we gave a call for specific types of healings, and six people were in the line who wanted salvation and deliverance from drugs, homosexuality, lesbianism and other evil spirits! They could not even wait until the salvation call at the end, that's why we stand ready with the sickle at all times to harvest the crop that is ripe and ready today!

On an Alaska trip, Charles rode in a cab (with a lady cabdriver) to one of our meeting places to set up our books for a night meeting. The fare was approximately $8.00 and Charles had purposed in his heart that it wasn't going to be spent for nothing, so he began sharing about the miracle-working power of God, and the woman accepted Jesus as her Savior and Lord before they reached the meeting place.

He set up the books, hailed another cab to bring him back, and this time he put his sickle out to harvest a man.

The man was from Romania and did not speak the best of English, but the Holy Spirit communicated a message to him and he prayed to receive Jesus before Charles got back to the hotel. Again, one soul — cost $8.00 plus Holy Spirit boldness!

At three minutes to ten, Charles was standing in the little enclosure leading to the entrance of an Alaskan bank, and a young man was standing with him, smoking a cigarette. Charles looked at the clock and decided there wasn't enough time to witness, but God spoke and said, "If you don't speak to him right now, there may never be another opportunity for him!" The clock had ticked off another minute, and now it was TWO minutes to ten.

Charles began speaking double time, and before the bank door opened, this young man asked Jesus to come into his heart and live His life through him! That's making the most of every minute!

Recently as we were returning from Denver, a distinguished looking man sat down next to us on a plane. We started a conversation concerning Jesus and were delighted to discover that he was a Christian, as well as a fund raiser for a large university specializing in research.

Among other things, he shared with us that their next project was an exciting one to feed the world. We asked him how they were going to do this, and he shared an interesting concept with us. He said it would be done by injecting bacteria into wood pulp, cardboard, cellulose and items of this nature, then injecting vitamins and flavoring into the product. The bacteria growth would cause the product to multiply and from this seemingly uncomplicated process there would be sufficient life-sustaining products to feed the world!

The minute he mentioned the multiplication process, Charles said, "Jesus and the loaves of bread!" The man said, "Yes!"

Instantly our minds went back to something that both of our mothers did! They made sour dough bread, and each time they pinched off a little piece and put it in a "starter" jar, so that the next time they would have the necessary leaven to start another batch! Was God speaking to us about the speed-up processes to make it possible to feed the world by supernatural accelerated multiplication?

"When it was evening, His disciples came to Him, saying, 'This is a deserted place, and the hour is already late. Send the multitudes away, that they may go into the villages and buy themselves food.' But Jesus said to them, 'They do not need to go away. You give them something to eat.' And they said to Him, 'We have here only five loaves and two fish.' He said, 'Bring them here to Me.' Then He commanded the multitudes to sit down on the grass. And He took the five loaves and the two fish, and looking up to heaven, He blessed and broke and gave the loaves to the disciples; and the disciples gave to the multitudes. So they all ate and were filled, and they took up twelve baskets full of the fragments that remained. Now those who had eaten were about five thousand men, besides women and children" (Matthew 14:15-21).

How did Jesus multiply that small portion of bread and fish? There had to be a supernatural process involved which speeded up the reproduction of the bread so that it would not be limited to five loaves, but a sufficient quantity to feed all those who were there, and have more left over than Jesus started with.

For many years we have stated and believed that the
world will never be fed by taking up offerings and sending
food overseas. This is good, because it is the only solution
we have at the present time, but we believe beyond a
shadow of doubt that in order for the world to be fed and
sustained, it will have to be through a supernatural process
of God. We feed the hungering today, and tomorrow they
feel the same hunger pangs again, but is there a way that
God could deliver a food with eternal sustaining power?

God fed Elijah in a supernatural way when He
commanded the ravens to feed him. The ravens brought
him bread and meat in the morning, and bread and meat in
the evening; and he drank from the brook. This was a
supernatural miracle but he needed sustenance twice daily,
just like we need our daily bread. (I Kings 17:4-6).

*"...suddenly an angel touched him, and said to him,
'Arise and eat.' Then he looked and there by his head was a
cake baked on coals, and a jar of water. So he ate and
drank, and lay down again. And the angel of the Lord
came back the second time, and touched him, and said,
'Arise and eat, because the journey is too great for you.'*

*"So he arose, and ate and drank; and he went in the
strength of that food forty days and forty nights as far as
Horeb, the mountain of God"* (I Kings 19:5-8).

God does things differently to accomplish whatever
He wants done. In the second story of Elijah, the angel fed
him twice and it was sufficient to sustain him for forty days
and nights while he was expending energy walking.

For forty years God fed the children of Israel manna
from heaven on a daily basis, and except for the sabbath it
only lasted for the one day.

In this end generation will God again rain down

manna from heaven as he did in days of old? Will he
send the ravens to feed the hungry of the world? Will he
send an angel or hosts of angels to feed every forty
days? Will we, like Jesus, multiply loaves and fishes to
feed the multitudes? Or will he allow us to use a simple
method known to all of us, and add a supernatural
pinch of power to make it possible through injecting
living bacteria into cellulose or a starter of sour dough
into a small amount of flour and see it accelerate in
increasing the loaves?

Is God saying that one of the greater end-time
things we will do is to feed a million people at one time,
rather than five thousand, and it will satisfy the physical
needs of the people over long periods of time, rather
than for one meal at a time?

Jesus used mighty miracles as His tools to cause
people to believe in Him. We believe He will transmit to
us, the Body of Christ, in this generation mighty power
to do greater things than He did to win whole cities and
nations to Him!

CHAPTER 20

YOU SPEAKA DA RUSSIAN
By Charles

We have told you scores of God's supernatural miracles which have happened in our own lives and ministry. There have been so many that it is not possible to recall but a scattering few because God is pouring out of His Spirit so mightily in this end of the end generation before the return of Jesus.

The miracles are increasing daily in such magnitude that we can hardly keep up with what Jesus is doing to prepare the church. He is speeding up the harvest of souls so that we believe millions will soon be coming into the Kingdom of God and really meaning it when they give their lives to Him.

We were sharing a small portion of this panorama of miracles in Birmingham, Alabama, in a Sunday afternoon miracle service on August 29, 1982. For the first time after God quickened my spirit to the fact that we could shift gears from the natural into the supernatural, we summarized the story with greater belief than anytime before. We said:

"We WILL move into a greater dimension of the supernatural than ever before.

"We WILL walk on physical water when God tells us to go to the other side to win someone or many to Jesus.

"We WILL translate to someplace like North Russia.

"We WILL speak to them in their native languages and feed great multitudes, and see them ALL saved, baptized with the Holy Spirit, healed, and sent forth as a mighty army to win their nation to Jesus!"

We were referring to the Body of Christ when we said WE, but we know that we will be among those being used by Jesus for this end generation wrap-up.

We had planned to stay in Birmingham that night and drive the approximate 200 miles to Chattanooga, Tennessee, the next morning. We did not have a speaking engagement until the next night. But Frances said, "Charles, I feel that we should drive on over there tonight."

I am learning to respond when God begins to deal with Frances, so I said, "Let's go." We packed our books and loaded them into the car and left about seven o'clock for Chattanooga. We listened to cassette tapes, we sang praises to God for his mighty miracles, we talked about Jesus, and were enjoying a pleasant drive.

I have always mentally computed the speedometer reading at the destination of a trip and so I added the mileage to the reading and determined what it would be when we got to Chattanooga. I can always know where we are in relation to the destination.

We were driving 55 miles an hour on the freeway about 11:30 that night, wide awake but anxious to get to bed after a long day from Houston to Birmingham, a miracle service, and then about a five-hour drive that night.

Frances was watching the road signs and suddenly we said excitedly, "CHATTANOOGA, 33 MILES!" We said, "Praise the Lord, we are almost there." I looked at the speedometer reading and it showed by my calculations that we were 34 miles from town.

It seemed as if we drove around a curve on the freeway, and there was another road sign which read, "CHATTANOOGA, 8 MILES!" Frances jumped up in the seat to look back at the sign we had just seen and said, "The road must have been under construction and they put the wrong sign up. But then I checked the speedometer and we had traveled 25 miles in a split-second.

Frances looked at me and said, "Did I fall asleep?" I answered her and said, "If you did, I did too, and if I had fallen asleep we would have wrecked the car." We dropped the subject, and it really seemed strange, but we drove the eight miles to Chattanooga, checked into the hotel and with still an unusual feeling we went to sleep.

We talked about this the first thing the next morning, and throughout the day, wondering what happened. I think we both knew we had translated the 25 miles, but we were hesitant to say it to each other until we had pondered it in our hearts awhile. Peter pondered in his heart for probably three days when God showed him the vision of the unclean things on the sheet let down from heaven before he fully realized what God meant.

By the second day, there was no doubt in our hearts that God had translated us, car, books, luggage and all!

We looked back in the Bible about Philip translating and discovered that he probably translated about 20 miles and didn't even have a car, books, and luggage with him. Jesus is the same yesterday, today, and forever! Hallelujah!

We added this translation miracle to some of the others we have shared with you in this book and have told the story of this end-time ministry of Jesus by the power of the Holy Spirit to many congregations across the United States.

In October, 1982, we were on the PTL Club satellite and shared this story for about thirty minutes.

Toward the end of the satellite program, I summarized the revelation and what we know by faith is about to happen before the return of Jesus.

I said something like, "We WILL translate into some foreign country like North Russia. We WILL speak in their native language to great hosts of people and they will understand what we are saying without an interpreter." Then I spoke briefly in tongues. I continued, "Then by the power of the Holy Spirit we WILL supernaturally feed these great multitudes with a heavenly food which will satisfy their physical needs. When they have finished eating all they want, we WILL simply wave our hands over the multitudes and they will all be healed.

"With very little preaching, but simply by the power of the Holy Spirit, we will present the Gospel of

Jesus to them and they will ALL be saved, they will ALL fall under the power of God, they will ALL begin to speak with other tongues as the Holy Spirit gives the utterance and will be endued with mighty power.

"They will be so touched by God and by His mighty miracles that they will BOLDLY spread like wildfire through their whole nation and great hosts through the nation will accept Jesus as their Savior and Lord. Nothing will be able to stop this mighty, power-filled army of believers.

We believe this is what Jesus will do to make the final preparation for His arrival for His church, and the scripture will come to pass: *"And this gospel of the kingdom will be preached in all the world as a witness to all the nations, AND THEN THE END WILL COME"* (Matthew 24:14).

We had just finished the program on satellite when a woman broke out of the audience and came running as fast as she could to the stage where we were ministering. There was such determination in her run that an air of expectancy arose over the entire audience. She grabbed me, hugged me, squeezed me, kissed me, and then backed off a step or two and pointed excitedly at me and said, "YOU SPEAKA DA RUSSIAN! YOU SPEAKA DA RUSSIAN! YOU SAY, 'YOU ARE DA SWEET MUDDA'S MILK FOR DA CHILDREN!'"

The Spirit of God fell like a bolt of lightning, and if there was any doubt in the minds of any of the audience, all doubt was removed when this Russian woman spoke words which we believe came like manna from heaven. We could not see a dry eye in the audience that night! There was almost a wail arose from the audience as they burst into tears.

What is the most nourishing and perfect food in all the world? Mother's milk!

Who are the hungry children? The new babies in Christ Jesus who were just born again!

God had supernaturally confirmed what He had told us about this end-time revival which will win whole nations to Jesus before His soon return! Glory to our Mighty God and to His Royal Son, Jesus!

Shortly after the PTL Club miracle, we received a call from Ron Smith, the manager of the radio station where we air our daily program. He is also an ordained minister of the Gospel, one seasoned in the Word and mature in Christ Jesus. Ron said he had a vision from the Lord for us and our ministry, but that he must share it personally with us instead of by phone.

He came to our home and shared this remarkable vision. He had not heard us share the story we have shared with you in this book, and only knows us casually. He had written the words of the vision and read them to us; we taped them and transcribed the message from God, and want to share it with you:

I would like to read the vision that the Lord gave me on Tuesday, November 23, 1982, while teaching at the Coral Ridge Training Center.

It was during this interim of teaching that I saw an "open" vision and it concerned the impending ministries of Charles and Frances Hunter. I witnessed the Shekinah presence of God lifting them literally off of the altar of the sacrifice of praise. As they were elevated above the earth's stratosphere, the Lord began to show me the next phase of their multi-faceted ministry.

First of all, I saw the Lord hand Charles and Frances a set of keys. Then I saw spiritually unborn nations. Each key unlocked a particular ministry.

These keys were all in a cluster on a beautiful golden chain, and that golden chain had engraved on it "END-TIME KEYS."

The first key was labeled "HEALING." I saw their ministries and I saw them crossing into countries in the international time zone and reaching into distant lands. I saw them ministering healing and the Word of God in countries that were steeped in witchcraft, superstition and humanism.

Then Revelation 22, verse 2, leaped out to me and I saw it as you would look at a ticker tape in a stock-market and that verse stated, "The leaves are for the healing of the nations." And then I understood what this first key was and its significance. The Hunters are going to bring the healing ministries of the Lord Jesus Christ into as yet spiritually unborn nations.

Then I saw the keys labeled "MIRACLES AND POWERS." And then I witnessed their words inspired by the Holy Spirit smashing against unyielding iron gates. And in my spirit I asked, "What are these gates?" as these gates literally BURST ASUNDER under the power of the Word of God. And the Spirit of God said to me, "These are the literal gates of hell and they are being penetrated, invaded and plundered by their ministry."

Then I saw Sister Frances and I saw her ministry as it would take on new horizons. And then I saw a key loom up and that key was captioned "BOLDNESS." This key is going to unlock yet many more doors in the days ahead. This key of boldness is a key of total confidence which has enabling abilities which will persuade heads of state to OPEN THEIR NATION and their doors to the futherance of the Gospel.

I saw another key and it was "THE PRINTED WORD" and it was in book and cassette form, and as a result the Hunter books will escalate to unprecedented dimensions and will become best sellers.

Charles, I saw some keys. These keys were very unique. One key was labeled "A WILLING PEN." And then the Lord showed me your tongue, and your tongue will be as the "pen of a ready writer". Deep stirrings in your inner man will enable you to teach the masses distinctly and put these words down where they can read it and interpret it as it is given out of your spirit. It will be a distinct, clear, and convincing message of Truth.

Also I saw another key, and it was "FULL BORN." I said, "What is this?" And then he showed me the gifts of the Spirit that both of you will teach, and the gifts of the Spirit will become "full born" in your own bosoms and the Holy Spirit will draw whatsoever gift he requires out of your spirits enabling you to do the Master's business!

Oh, it was wonderful as God would show these keys to me as I was teaching just a regular group of people in this particular setting.

And then as I was waiting before the Lord to see if there would be anything more, he spoke to me, and he said, "This is only the first phase of their end-time new dimensional ministry. I have much more to disclose and to confirm in the months ahead to the Hunters," that he will through yielded vessels.

Then Ron began to speak to us and said, "Charles the amazing thing in this that the Lord showed me was that I was just teaching along and this vision just 'BOOM' happened, and I never did stop teaching the people. I began to teach out of the mental realm while out of the spirit this is all going on!

"And I saw this altar of sacrifice, and it's the whole burnt offering where that altar is, and we know that is the sweet savour unto God. Both of you had so committed and dedicated your lives unto the Lord that he could take all of you. A lot of times we are not totally there, but the both of you are on that altar totally yielded to God, and so he could do with you whatever he wanted to do. Yielded!

"This cloud which lifted you up was a telecommunications glory cloud; it was the Shekinah cloud of God. All kinds of communication rays were shooting out of it, and were going everywhere. This cloud had the telecommunication powers in it so that it is going to go to all five continents."

The conversation was then accelerated by a message in tongues by Ron's wife, Carol, and interpreted by Ron.

My kingly scepter is extended to you because you have found favor in my presence just as Esther of old, and as a result, she was the Savior of sorts even to her own people. But I will create you in the same dimensions where that you will come before kings, even though they are ungodly, and they shall extend the scepter unto you and you shall receive the power, their power, and their words to go into their country and to establish my kingdom of righteousness and the vision that I have given will be actually carried out and it shall come to pass and IT IS WELL INTO ITS OPERATION PERIOD.

As I pondered on this vision which God had given to Ron Smith, and reflected on the possibility of my "tongue as the pen of a ready writer", I saw another of the end-time ways Jesus might use to get the message to all the earth before His return.

In my spirit I saw words coming out of my mouth instantly being supernaturally imprinted on paper which would be used and studied by the new converts. This would simply be done by the power of God without the benefit of a printing press. I could see the Soviet police grabbing the papers out of their hands to put them in prison for reading Bible literature, and the papers turning to ashes in their hands right in front of their very eyes! What do you think that would do to the police? I believe they would be born again right on the spot because they would have seen the supernatural power of God!

Simultaneously as that thought flashed through my mind, I remembered Pastor Buck telling about the 120 future events which God told him would happen as a confirmation to him that he was actually in heaven. He said it wasn't like you and I write; the information just suddenly appeared. He continued and said, "I did not even need to read it, but right now, I can tell you EVERYTHING that was on that paper, because it was instantly impressed on my mind like a printing press prints on paper. The press doesn't have to read what is imprinted. It's there! In the same way, every single notation was burned into my mind, and it's still there!"

When Pastor Buck returned to earth, the paper was still in his hand, so he laid it on his desk in his office, went home to tell his wife what had happened, and when he returned, the paper had turned to ashes! Many people saw them, and they finally disintegrated!

Look at the parallel with the believers in Russia! Even though the police might grab the papers out of their hands, the information would be imprinted on their minds.

Supernatural? Yes, but everything about God and Jesus is supernatural, so when we believe in them, we have to believe in the supernatural!

Since August, 1982, God has been revealing to us some of the end-time ministry for the Body of Christ, and He has not only chosen us, but also YOU to prepare for His return.

We want you to go with us into this new realm which promises to include those things Jesus was talking about when He said, *"Most assuredly, I say to you, he who believes in Me, the works that I do he will do also; and greater works than these he will do, because I go to My Father"* (John 14:12).

While we are led by the Holy Spirit and not by prophecy, this vision confirms what God has been telling us and which he has already started doing in our ministry. Be alert with us to the miracles of the first Church when the first disciples translated, walked on water, raised the dead and did many other unusual signs. We are the end-generation and you and we are the disciples whom God will use to do the miracles of greater magnitude to win the lost by the millions in this final harvest of souls.

Keep this vision in mind so we can watch God fulfill it together.

CHAPTER 21

IT'S BEGINNING TO RAIN
By Charles

God is moving so rapidly we can hardly keep up with Him. On Monday, September 20, 1982, I had a supernatural visitation from the Lord in the form of a vision.

IT'S BEGINNING TO RAIN!

It is 3:26 o'clock in the morning as I write this because God just gave me a vision that stirred my heart and I began to weep. God said, "Write it now!"

I saw a farmer admiring his bountiful crop of grain which was extremely beautiful. He had worked hard all year, and now, finally his work was almost complete and his grain was glistening in the sunlight as he prepared to bring in the combines the next morning to start harvesting the greatest bumper crop he had ever seen. He was so proud and happy about this field of beauty.

God said, "This is likened to the Kingdom of Heaven except that instead of Jesus saying it to the early Church, He is saying it now to the disciples of this end-

time Church.''

The farmer was wiping the sweat off his brow and the heat of the fall months didn't bother him at all because he saw in his farmer spirit the tons and tons of this rich grain already in the bins, and he was very pleased.

Suddenly he felt a breeze begin to blow. In what seemed only moments to him, it blew stronger and stronger, and then he saw clouds beginning to form. He was a farmer and he knew the signs of rain, and fear struck him as he realized that it was beginning to sprinkle.

He began to run toward the house to get help and saw his neighbor. He yelled with all his voice, "COME, COME HERE AND HELP ME! THE RAIN IS GOING TO RUIN MY BEAUTIFUL GRAIN AND I NEED HELP. HELP!!! HELP!!! HELP!!!

But his neighbor yelled back, "I NEED HELP, TOO! COME QUICKLY!"

The farmer saw other neighbors, but all of them had the same problem because all the farms had billions of grains and it had to be gathered NOW or it would be too late!

It was a sudden storm, totally unexpected, and it came fiercely! It was beginning to rain harder and harder and even some sleet came down and the farmer could do nothing. It was horrible!

He stood watching, but could do absolutely nothing. He was completely helpless. The sleet was not noticeable as it pelted his face, and his tears came pouring down almost like the streams of rain, because ALL HE HAD - EVERYTHING was being destroyed in *minutes right before his eyes!*

Then the rains stopped, almost as suddenly as they had started, and the silence was so great that it was like the whole world had come to a sudden halt, and everything in God's creation became silent. Not a sound could be heard except the weeping of the farmer, but it was too late! TOO LATE! IT WAS GONE! IT WAS ALL GONE!

Then in my vision God said, "This is the end age in which you are living right now. You are the disciples of this generation and the work must be done quickly or it will be too late."

He reminded me of the billions of souls around the world who don't know Jesus, and showed me a flashback of the billions of grains on the stalks, ready for harvest. He said He needed help. He depends upon His people to do ALL the harvesting. He has hosts of angels working, but they are sent as fellow-servants to help.

God said as a reminder of the plea of Jesus, "The harvest truly is great, but the laborers are few; therefore pray the Lord of the harvest to send out laborers into His harvest" (Luke 10:2).

God showed this so clearly to me in the vision that my whole body shook because of the weeping when the realization was made so vivid that it's beginning to rain, Rain, RAIN, and that WE are the harvesters of this final crop. It is a bumper crop and the people all over the world are so ready to accept Jesus, but God said even His believers are too busy looking at their bounty, even the bountiful knowledge of the Word, that they are not alert to the ready fields, and the rains are coming suddenly as a thief in the night. It will be too late unless the course is changed NOW.

God said, "Cry out to the other Christians and tell them as loudly as you can yell, 'HELP, HELP, HELP! ALL IS GOING TO BE LOST.'" Then he continued and said, "But yet there is a little time left and I will call upon my people and they will respond and I have sent great hosts of angels from heaven to aid in this final great harvest. I don't want any of them to perish!"

We are the disciples of this end generation and it is almost over. If we are going to do our job like the disciples of the first Church, we must do it NOW with so much urgency that we will get the grain gathered before it is too late!

CHAPTER 22

PURGING FIRE, PURITY AND COMPASSION
By Frances

We could not close the final pages of this book without sharing some excitement about fire which has happened four times in the last three weeks in our ministry.

First it was Fort Walton Beach, Florida. We had shared about SUPERNATURAL HORIZONS and the congregation grasped the vision of what God is doing in these end times. God is not going to use the sin-stained life to accomplish His end-time ministry, but He is looking for those who are willing to live a holy life, spotless and without a wrinkle or blemish, and even those who are willing to be hated and persecuted for Jesus' sake! He is looking for people who will lift their eyes above the normal, nitty-gritty problems of daily living and look into the supernatural instead of at themselves!

In his book, ELIJAH, PROPHET OF POWER (Word Books, Publisher), W. Phillip Keller says, "The instant God diverts an individual's attention from his or her own petty problems and self-centered little interests, to the great power of His own person, there are potentials for enormous exploits under the impetus of God's energy. Most of us block the movement of God's Spirit not only in our own lives, but also in the world at large, by our own selfish intransigence.

"The hour that Elijah crawled out of his cave of self-pity and sad introspection was a turning point in his walk with God. As he stood erect on the great mount in full view of his God, his eyes were lifted to see far horizons of exciting new adventures."

God is looking for people who will respond spontaneously! He is looking for people who will look outward and upward instead of inward. As we gave this call, almost the entire congregation came forward. We all lifted our hands in worship and praise, we sang in English, we sang in the Spirit, we prayed in English, and we prayed in the Spirit. Then the praise lifted to higher levels and we began to sing that beautiful anointed song, "We Shall Behold Him!" The power and the presence of God was almost beyond the capability of the human mind to understand or the human body to experience.

As this high praise was being ministered heavenward, I looked at Charles and was astonished and amazed! It appeared as though he had been drenched in gasoline and set on fire. Extending out from his entire body from head to toe were flames of fire about eighteen inches long. They were not flames that were going up as a fire usually burns, but flames which were extending outward as if to reach the entire congregation with a baptism of fire to burn out all the dross in every life. Charles reminded me of the burning bush in the Bible! The flames of Pentecost were blazing forth from one who had received the power of the Holy Spirit!

I pointed to Charles and as I did, I noticed that my arm was blazing the same as Charles' was, and as I looked down, I saw that my entire body was also flaming with the same kind of fire, reaching out to the audience!

God spoke to me and said, "Lay hands on all those who are willing to commit their lives totally to me FOR THE BAPTISM WITH FIRE!"

Charles and I went through this great host of disciples of this end generation of believers and the power of God fell upon them. Angels came and began to touch the heads of the people as God displayed His glory in a way we had never seen before.

We are in the end church age and God is going to be exploding His miracle work on earth like never before in the history of the world. We are blessed to be living in the most exciting time ever...but that's not all!

The next "fire" experience occurred in Maui, Hawaii just a week later at the First Assembly of God Church. They hold their meetings in a huge roller skating rink and on the next-to-the-last night we called the entire congregation forward. During the week there had been many exciting conversions of drug addicts, "free sex" advocates, alcoholics and many others, and the faith which had built up was beautiful to behold in an atmosphere of the world's population of Japanese, Hawaiian, Chinese, German, Portugese, French, Spanish, English, and almost every nationality you could think of!

As the entire group surged forward, someone began to sing in the Spirit, and everyone joined in. It was like the waves of the sea as it swelled and diminished, then swelled again and again. The presence of God enveloped everyone there and took them almost literally out of this world.

A woman ran out of the audience to a couple who had gone to Hawaii with us, and she said, "I'm afraid, I'm afraid!" The man said, "What are you afraid of?" She said, "That huge blanket of fire which is covering the entire audience!"

Again, God had manifested His supernatural power by sending fire!

But there's more...and it happened two days later at the First Assembly of God Church in Honolulu. Again it occurred as we began singing in tongues at the end of the service! Almost the entire church fell under the power of God, and angels dropped healing on approximately 200 people as Charles led a prayer of healing and waved his hands across the audience. It was reported that a huge angel had stood behind Charles and me during the entire service, sometimes with his arm around one of us and sometimes around the other. But the most spectacular thing was that rays of light were seen behind us during most of the service and at the very end, brilliant flashes of lightning raced back and forth across the entire audience.

"His glory covered the heavens,
And the earth was full of His praise,
His brightness was like the light;
He had rays flashing from His hand,

And there His power was hidden"
(Habakkuk 3:3,4).
Just like it happened in the Word of God, it is happening today!

Could it be that as we are seeing fire and light more often in our services, the praise, worship, and prayers of the people are becoming the keys to opening the doorway into a portion of the dimension of eternity?

Is travailing in intercession, walking closely with God, living a holy life, believing what Jesus said we would be able to do without limitations, walking in the light as He is in the light, the breakthrough from the limited dimension of the flesh into the limitlessness of the spirit world?

Can the radiation of the light and power of God within Spirit-filled worshippers be given out so freely and powerfully that whole audiences will be flashing light? Can the presence of God be so dramatically demonstrated in services like the ones we have described that even whole audiences who are in the Spirit will translate into far away places to multiply the ministry of the Gospel? Can the magnitude of such mass ministry be so vast that whole nations will receive the Gospel at almost instant speed?

Can we intercede in prayer and praise, praying with our understanding and praying with our spirits, so effectively that we will move between flesh and spirit as though we are living in two worlds? Pastor Buck testified of doing that, and Paul testified of doing it. Pastor Buck said it was as though he lived in two worlds, not knowing which one he was in or which one he preferred. Are we re-enacting the book of Acts, but in even greater ways?

God is light, Jesus is the light of the world, and He said we are the light of the world, God is a consuming fire, so why shouldn't fire and light be manifested when they are present!

We have not heard much from the Body of Christ about fire and the baptism with fire in this generation, but in these last days we will see more and more manifestations of God's glory and His purging power to perfect the saints.

Ezekiel described his visions of God, and fire or smoke was present when the glory of God was present. *"Then I looked, and behold, a whirlwind was coming out of the north, a great cloud with raging fire engulfing itself; and brightness was all around it and radiating out of its midst like the color of amber, out of the midst of the fire"* (Ezekiel 1:4).

As for the likeness of the living creatures, their appearance was like burning coals of fire, and like the appearance of torches. Fire was going back and forth among the living creatures; the fire was bright, and out of the fire went lightning. And the living creatures ran back and forth, in appearance like a flash of lightning" (Ezekiel 1:13, 14).

And above the firmament over their heads was the likeness of a throne, in appearance like a sapphire stone; on the likeness of the throne was a likeness with the appearance of a man high above it. Also from the appearance of His waist and upward I saw, as it were, the color of amber with the appearance of fire all around within it; and from the appearance of His waist and downward I saw, as it were, the appearance of fire with brightness all around. Like the appearance of a rainbow in a cloud on a rainy day, so was the appearance of the brightness all around it. This was the appearance of the likeness of the glory of the Lord" (Ezekiel 1:26-28).

"For our God is a consuming fire" (Hebrews 12:29).

"John answered, saying to them all, 'I indeed baptize you with water; but one mightier than I is coming, whose sandal strap I am not worthy to loose. He will baptize you with the Holy Spirit AND WITH FIRE" (Luke 3:16).

"Now when the Day of Pentecost had fully come, they were all with one accord in one place. And suddenly there came a sound from heaven, as of a rushing mighty wind, and it filled the whole house where they were sitting. Then there appeared to them DIVIDED TONGUES, AS OF FIRE, and one sat upon each of them" (Acts 2:1-3).

We believe fire will be seen very frequently as the Spirit of God moves more and more mightily in these last days. God cannot stand sin, not even little sins, because He is calling His people to be holy, without spot, blemish, or wrinkle.

When we are to be used in this generation as a disciple of Jesus, we must be holy as He is holy; we must not be lukewarm lest He spew us out of His mouth.

We believe we must clean up our lives to operate in the righteousness of God before the supernatural, such as translations, will be a part of God's use for us. Look at Enoch and the reason he was translated: *"By faith Enoch was translated, so that he did not see death, 'and*

WAS NOT FOUND BECAUSE God had translated him', for BEFORE his translation he had this testimony, THAT HE PLEASED GOD. But without faith it is impossible to please Him, for he who comes to God must believe that He is, and that He is a rewarder of THOSE WHO DILIGENTLY SEEK HIM" (Hebrews 11:5, 6).

Once the early disciples received the power of the Holy Spirit, we see them living a holy life and being willing to do anything necessary to uplift the name of Jesus at the sacrifice of even their own lives. That we must be willing to do, to be used of God in the dimension of the supernatural about which we are talking!

Before Jesus comes back, the Body of Christ must be united in love. As we draw closer and closer to His return, we will find one of the supernatural manifestations will be the strong bonds of love that will bind us together...from all denominations, from all differences of opinion...from all strife, bitterness, hatred and the other tools of Satan which will try to keep us from being one with Christ Jesus in His powerful God love.

"Since you have PURIFIED YOUR SOULS IN OBEYING THE TRUTH through the Spirit in sincere LOVE of the brethen, LOVE one another fervently with a pure heart, having been born again, not of corruptible seed but incorruptible, through the Word of God which lives and abides forever..." (I Peter 1:22, 23).

"Behold what manner of love the Father has bestowed on us, that we should be called children of God!" (I John 3:1); *"And everyone who has this hope in*

Him purifies himself, just as He is pure" (I John 3:3); *"Beloved, let us love one another, for love is of God; and everyone who loves is born of God and knows God. He who does not love does not know God, for God is love. In this the love of God was manifested toward us, that God has sent His only begotten Son into the world, that we might live through Him. In this is love, not that we loved God, but that He loved us and sent His Son to be the propitiation for our sins. Beloved, if God so loved us, we also ought to love one another"* (I John 4:7-11).

"Now, Lord, look on their threats, and grant to Your servants that with all boldness they may speak Your Word, by stretching out Your hand to heal, and that signs and wonders may be done through the name of Your holy servant Jesus."

"And when they had prayed, the place where they were assembled together was shaken; and they were all filled with the Holy Spirit, and they spoke the Word of God with boldness" (Acts 4:29-31).

In Fresno, California an unusual thing happened. We were in the home of pastor Tom Tiemens and his wife, and were holding their hands, asking God to transfer to them any anointing and gifts of ours which they did not already have in their supernatural ministry. We often feel the flow of the power of the Holy Spirit moving from our hands into those to whom we are ministering, but this time the energy was swiftly flowing simultaneously from us through their hands and from their hands through ours. Frances said it felt to her as if there were layers of power flowing both ways; to me it felt like the streams of power were merging as they flowed in both directions. It didn't meet head-on like a collision.

It reminded me of the way Dr. Richard Eby described a scene when he was in heaven, walking through beautiful flowers about two feet high. He wondered if he was trampling them down, so he looked as he walked through them and saw that his feet and legs went through the flowers, and the flowers went through his feet and legs!

We felt God was saying that His love and unity will flow in an uninterrupted current between those who give their all to Him as we finalize this era.

Another major area of entering into the great supernatural spirit world in the end times will be through intercessory prayer. *"Confess your trespasses to one another, and pray for one another, that you may be healed. The effective fervent prayer of a righteous man avails much"* (James 5:16).

Our brother Kenneth Copeland shared after sixteen days in meditation with God the first of 1983, that the disciples entered into a new dimension as they interceded for boldness, and that we must do the same to do God's miracles in this generation.

We feel that intercessory prayer and compassion will be keys to unlock the door to translation and other dimensions of the spirit world. When we get so concerned that we will intercede for hours because of our compassion for the souls of people, God will take us supernaturally to those people to minister life to them.

Paul travailed as a woman in labor for the ones about whom he was deeply concerned. *"My little children, for whom I labor* (travail) *in birth again until Christ is formed in you, I would like to be present with you right now and to change my tone; for I have doubts about you"* (Galatians 4:19, 20).

A pastor friend of ours called this week to say that he had travailed for us during the past three or more weeks. He said he actually hurt inside physically and could not get a release from intercession for us. We had been going through major changes in our ministry which from the fleshly standpoint were bad, but in the Spirit realm were exciting because we had heard from God. It was through his and other intercession that we were able to maintain perfect peace and excitement about the whole situation. We must be able to enter into intercession for one another and for the work of God in order to stay in the Spirit and not in the flesh.

CHAPTER 23

A BOOK THAT CAN NEVER END
By Frances

Some books are difficult to write — but this one is difficult to conclude because God continues to accelerate the supernatural in our services and we have an urging to include some extra supernatural "goodies" which have happened, with possibly some extra thoughts which have come into our minds as we have proofed the final copy of SUPERNATURAL HORIZONS.

One such extra was information given to us by a converted, Spirit-filled Jew, who told the story of translation as it concerns the veil of the temple!

The temple of God in the Old Testament was shielded from everyone except the High Priest, and he could only go into the Holy of Holies once a year. This he did by going through the thick veil which separated God's presence from the sins of the world.

This veil stood between sinful man and God until that great day when *"Jesus cried out with a loud voice, and breathed His last. THEN THE VEIL OF THE*

TEMPLE WAS TORN IN TWO FROM TOP TO BOTTOM" (Mark 15:37, 38).

Jesus opened the heavenly doorway for each of us to go into the very presence of the Almighty God and personally talk with Him, using the name of Jesus as our passport. He is our High Priest and is the supernatural doorway into God's presence.

The veil was a thick, heavy curtain with no openings. Did you ever wonder how the High Priests in the Old Testament got behind the veil? Actually this thought never crossed our minds until just recently when we were sharing about translation and someone mentioned that the only way they could have gotten through the veil was by translating!

This was confirmed by this converted Jew who was previously in the priesthood. He shared that there are two ways God's laws are passed down to Jews. One is the written law, which is the Old Testament; the other is the spoken word, where it is verbally passed from generation to generation. One such spoken word is that the High Priest "translated" through the veil when he entered once a year! Glory to God!

What will God do next to display His glory and His power in the twentieth century?

We don't know, but one thing we do know is that He will bring about soon all the things He has told us and which we have shared in this book, and MUCH, MUCH MORE!

Even this morning, Charles was awakened by a dream which was so real that he feels God is further preparing us for the great things He has ahead for all who live for Him.

In the dream, Charles shared that he had been speaking to an audience in an auditorium which was located in the end room of a large warehouse building. When he was making his final remarks, he walked through the audience, down a long corridor, out the front of the building, and made a quick turn to the side of the building. He said it was as though he started jogging when his steps grew longer and longer and then he realized he was moving into the air. It was awesome because he knew that was the beginning of translations through space in the physical body.

Still dreaming, Charles discovered himself in the air flying about twenty feet above the ground over his neighbor's back-yard garden where the wife was hoeing in her garden. From the air he said, "Do you know Jesus as your Savior?" He landed near her, and her husband came out and he was leading them to Jesus. He laid his hands on each of them and they went under the power in their garden, smiling because Jesus had become real to them.

Then he found himself again in the air flying with ease far above the rooftops of a residential area, realizing that once we break through the veil in translating, we can do it whenever necessary to get the Gospel of Jesus to someone who is seeking God, for He said if you seek Me, you will find Me!

When Charles awakened from the sleep during which this dream occurred, he felt for about twenty minutes that it was an actual happening and not a dream. Because of being involved constantly in the supernatural power of God, we are super sensitive to those times when special anointings come upon us. For some time after he awoke, there was an unusually heavy anointing of the Spirit upon him. It is for this reason that we believe this was a God-given dream to further prepare us for the dimension of the Spirit world into which we are moving. Or did he actually translate?

Just before going to press with this book, another exciting manifestation of the power of the Holy Spirit was demonstrated in Fresno, California.

We were in the great Civic Center Theater, and as we entered into the second night of ministry the worship and praise was reaching new heights toward God and Jesus.

It was during this time when we were glorifying Jesus and God that the glory of God came into the theater and filled it with a thin smoke. We drew this to the attention of the congregation, and then God opened my spirit eyes to see a most unusual and spectacular sight. The lower floor was mostly filled with people, but the balcony was not being occupied, and yet there was not an empty seat in the whole theater!

I had never before seen angels sitting, but this night every seat not occupied by people was filled by one of God's angels!

Then the gift of prophecy came forth through Pastor Tom Tiemens of the Belmont Believers Church in Fresno, in a powerful way as God spoke confirming the message we were to share, the story of this book, SUPERNATURAL HORIZONS FROM GLORY TO GLORY. Even before we began ministering, God announced through this prophecy what He thinks about this end-time message. People in the congregation told us that during this time the pastor and his wife, and Charles and I were approximately eighteen inches out of our bodies in what must have appeared to have been an elongated double vision!

Extracts of the prophecy are given here:

I am in the midst of My people tonight, and so I call upon you to lift your hands toward Heaven. I call upon you, says the Lord, to bless My Holy name and as you bless My name, then the glory of God shall fill the tabernacle, Yea, even the presence of My glory and the presence of My fire shall come upon you!

My Spirit, says the Lord, is calling in this hour. Who are those that will hear? Who are those that will give ear to the counsel of God? Who are those that shall bring themselves before Me? Who are those that shall humble themselves before Me? Who are those that will lay themselves prostrate in worship and in praise before Me?

Those are they who have made a decision to be sold out; those are they that have made a decision before Me to consecrate their hearts and their lives; those are they that hear the voice of My Spirit; those are they that love Me; those are they that have abandoned this world and all of the earthly pleasures to follow Me.

I desire to lead you out and on to a new glory and faith. I desire to guide you and to lead you into a new demonstration of My Spirit and My power. Will you come follow Me, you that love Me, you that have consecrated your lives before Me? Will you step into this new dimension of My glory; will you behold My salvation, will you behold those things that the prophets of old and the apostles of old longed to experience and to see into, for this is the hour that I desire to do a new thing among My people.

Men shall not be able to run nor shall they be able to hide from My glory, says the Lord, for My knowledge shall fill the earth. Yes, even My knowledge and My glory shall cover this earth as never before. There will be those that will harden their hearts against Me and say I don't want anything to do with this, and they shall run and hide and give themselves over to a reprobate mind. Oh, don't be like them, says the Lord. It is they that shall bring the wrath of God upon themselves. My grace and My mercy, yea, even My glory and My truth, are available in this hour and I'm calling unto My people to come walk with Me; come follow Me.

Step into the splendor and into the glory and into the majesty, into this thing that I desire to do in the earth, for it shall be the greatest revelation of My power, it shall be the greatest revelation of My glory that this world has ever experienced.

IT SHALL BE THE POWER AND MAJESTY THAT USHERS IN JESUS, SAYS THE LORD!

For you have not yet even begun to see My glory or My power in demonstration. Oh you've seen a glimpse here and yes, you've seen a glimpse there, but it is time and this is the hour that I have chosen for you to be a part of that which I have ushered into this hour.

It is time, saith the Lord, for My glory and My power to be demonstrated in the manner in which I have designed it to operate. But My children, hearken unto

My voice, hearken unto that which has been said and spoken to you. It is time for you to sound the alarm. It is time for you to hearken unto My voice. It is time for you to fall before Me, to worship Me, to praise Me, to pray and to seek Me, and to know that I am your God, and that I am all power, and that I am all glory, and that it is My desire to fulfill all that I have said I shall do! But hearken unto My voice, My children, for it is unto you that I have quickened you, it is unto you that I have placed it within your hands, for it is within you that My glory shall be demonstrated all around the earth; it is unto you that that glory and power shall be manifested through.

I am calling you even this moment. It is time for you to set yourself aright unto what the Spirit of God would have done in this day, in this moment, in this hour. Don't be afraid of what I do. Don't be afraid of My glory and the revelation of My power. It must come to pass, says the Lord.

Revival must come, says the Lord. The glory of the Lord must visit this earth before My Son returns. My power shall be in great display. Every nation, every kindred, every tongue shall be touched by My power.

There will be those who won't understand. There will be those who will fear the glory of the Lord. But I exhort you, do not be afraid of what I will do. For you shall see the manifestation of My power, and you shall see the manifestation of My glory, and great shall be My might upon the earth. Great shall be My might and great shall be My glory, and knees shall bow and tongues shall confess that Jesus is Lord and that I live in the heavens.

You are on the threshold of the greatest revival that

the world has ever seen. You are even at the door, says the Lord, of the latter rain of My Spirit, My power, and My fire. So when it comes, don't be afraid of it, and be reminded of the word that was delivered to you, says the Lord, for these things shall come to pass.

Jesus said to her, "Did I not say to you that if you would believe you would see the glory of God?"